LLOYD REES IN EUROPE

LLOYD REES IN EUROPE

SELECTED DRAWINGS FROM HIS SKETCHBOOKS
IN THE GALLERY'S COLLECTION

Hendrik Kolenberg

assisted by Patricia James

ART
GALLERY
NSW

Lloyd Rees painting on the Grand Canal, Venice, 1953 photograph by Alan Rees

Accompanying this publication is an exhibition: *Lloyd Rees, European sketchbooks and related works*
Art Gallery of New South Wales
9 February – 28 April 2002

© Art Gallery of New South Wales
Design by Mark Boxshall
Film by Spitting Image, Sydney
Printing by Samhwa Printing Co., Seoul

Cataloguing-in-publication data:
Rees, Lloyd, 1895–1988.

Lloyd Rees in Europe: selected drawings from his sketchbooks in the Gallery's collection / Hendrik Kolenberg assisted by Patricia James.

Includes bibliographic references.
ISBN 0734763271

1. Rees, Lloyd, 1895-1988 – Journeys – Europe – Exhibitions. 2. Rees, Lloyd, 1895-1988 – Notebooks, sketchbooks, etc. – Exhibitions. 3. Art Gallery of New South Wales – Exhibitions. 4. Europe in art – Exhibitions. I. Kolenberg, Hendrik. II. James, Patricia Mary. III. Art Gallery of New South Wales. IV. Title. V. Title: Lloyd Rees, European sketchbooks and related works.

Contents

Foreword

Since the showing of our popular *Lloyd Rees drawings, centenary retrospective*
exhibition in 1995 the Gallery has been given all of Lloyd Rees's nineteen
remaining sketchbooks, a particularly generous donation from Alan and Jancis Rees,
the artist's son and daughter-in-law.

Rees's sketchbooks are extraordinary for the quality and lively personality of his
draughtsmanship. Lloyd Rees was a natural and passionate draughtsman and the
spontaneity and momentary capture of these drawings evoke a wonderful sense of
time and place. This publication concentrates on the drawings Rees made on
several extended trips to Europe in the 1950s, 60s and 70s, when he was at the
height of his powers as a painter, greatly respected by his peers and his work keenly
sought after by private collectors and public galleries.

One hundred and ten drawings have been selected from almost 700 in his
sketchbooks, a task undertaken by Hendrik Kolenberg, Senior Curator of Australian
Prints, Drawings and Watercolours, who was responsible for the 1995 Rees
drawings exhibition. He has also organized the accompanying exhibition of Rees's
European sketchbook drawings and related works.

The Art Gallery of New South Wales has the most comprehensive collection of
Lloyd Rees's work, especially of his prints and drawings, largely due to the
generosity of the artist's son and daughter-in-law. They kindly placed all the prints
and drawings remaining after Lloyd Rees's death, with the Gallery for the purposes
of research and study and are presenting some as gifts for the permanent collection,
each year under the Cultural Gifts Programme.

Books on artist's sketchbooks are rare. There are certainly very few on
Australian artists. This publication is therefore special – a selection of what is in our
collection by one of the finest and most admired of all Australian artists.

Edmund Capon
Director

opposite: Lloyd Rees (in a hat) drawing in Venice,
surrounded by onlookers, 1953 photograph by Alan Rees

INTRODUCTION

At a time when more artists than ever turn to a camera for recording what interests them, or manipulate images photographically, Lloyd Rees's unassuming sketchbook drawings have a startling intensity, authenticity and spontaneity. They have the power to put you wherever he was – looking at and drawing something in particular, whether that is in Venice or San Gimignano, on the Spanish Steps in Rome, the waterfront at Mýkonos, along the Seine in Paris, or coastline from a ship. You can sense just what it is that interests him about a subject and why he was compelled to draw it. His drawings also awaken an interest in the places he visited, with him as guide.

Our increasing reliance upon the convenience of cameras and other mechanical aids, is such that we often have difficulty in recalling what we saw without them. The practice of drawing, which was a lifelong activity for Rees, sharpens the capacity to observe and to remember. It is the coordination between eyes, brain and hands which is miraculous and of which Rees's drawings in his European sketchbooks are such a good example.

In seeking out some of Rees's best known subjects in Paris in December 2000, I was struck by the inadequacy of recording photographically what he saw and drew. His drawings are invariably more accurate and memorable than any photograph. To study his drawings in relation to photographs of the subjects, beyond identifying a building, street or mountain, can be quite misleading.

Human sight is binocular, a camera is monocular. This alone distinguishes us, without taking into account that we instantaneously think, feel and act upon what we see as well. Lloyd Rees had an unerring capacity for translating the essentials of what he saw onto paper or canvas – spatial relationships, perspective and structure are unified in his drawings to create a convincing image of what was before him. We are fortunate that for his European subjects in particular, we can refer to drawings in sketchbooks that show us what initially attracted him to a subject, and to the painting or drawing that followed, thereby showing just what part they had in the evolution of his work.

Drawing from observation in sketchbooks emphasizes individual vision and the hand-made. Rees drew fastidiously but quickly in his sketchbooks, his handwriting, personality and emotion inextricably part of the activity. He rarely started a work without his subject matter before him – he was a passionate advocate of remaining true to first visual impressions. His European sketchbooks confirm and celebrate that and as a result provide us with the most intimate and revealing encounter with his work and its sources.

Artists' sketchbooks are often private and too rarely shown. They may be jealously guarded by him or her (or by an artist's family or descendents) as being too revealing, or the works in them considered too rudimentary. Yet, like diaries and letters, they are often valuable aids to better appreciating and understanding an artist's work. At the end of his life Lloyd Rees was anxious that the drawings that remained with him be kept together and find a place at the Art Gallery of New South Wales, with which he had a long and fruitful association. His sketchbooks are the first drawings from his estate to be gifted to the Gallery by Alan and Jan Rees, the artist's son and daughter-in-law. They are part of a remarkable legacy, invaluable for the study of Rees's work and the part drawing from observation plays in it.

Lloyd Rees's drawings of Europe in his extant sketchbooks from 1953 to 1973 are amongst the most interesting, numerous and sustained in quality by an Australian artist. They are remarkably modest in size by today's standards, but in the accuracy and immediacy of his draughtsmanship are also amongst his most irresistible and important works.

Rees's sketchbook drawings of Europe have not been considered separately from his other drawings before and relatively few (which he sold individually or which have been illustrated in books or exhibition catalogues) have previously been identified as such. There are almost 700 drawings remaining in his extant sketchbooks now in the Art Gallery of New South

opposite: Lloyd Rees, *Arezzo* 1959 (detail) p. 66 (45)

Wales collection, most of which are of Europe. Although Rees removed some drawings from his sketchbooks for sale, he kept his European sketchbooks largely intact as source material. The two sketchbooks from his visit to Europe with his wife Marjory in 1953, have not had any pages removed.

Rees did not own or ever use a camera, so his sketchbook drawings provided the record he needed of a place. He drew his subjects *in situ*, a time honoured and for Rees a life-long practice which began for him as an adolescent around 1913, when the streets and architecture of Brisbane where he was born, first seriously attracted his attention.[1]

Rees travelled to Europe for the first time in 1923 to meet his fiancée, sculptor Daphne Mayo. They had become engaged in the previous year. Like Rees, a former student of Brisbane Technical College, she had been in London since 1919, the recipient of the first Queensland Travelling Art Scholarship. Mayo completed her studies at the Royal Academy, London in 1923 and was awarded a gold medal for sculpture and another travelling scholarship, to Rome. From London Lloyd Rees travelled with Daphne Mayo to Paris and later to Rome. In 1924, Rees returned to Sydney. Much to his disappointment however, their engagement was broken off the following year, Daphne Mayo having decided to devote herself entirely to sculpture. [2]

During his time in England and Europe Rees produced many drawings and some paintings – which he exhibited in 1924 after his return to Australia – and developed an even greater appetite for European landscape and architecture than he had previously. This eventually led to extended return visits with his wife Marjory in 1953, 1959, 1966–67 and 1973.

From the extant sketchbooks it is possible to reconstruct Rees's travels in Europe, to follow his movements from place to place, sometimes day by day, especially when the drawings he removed and sold are taken into account. The exhibition which accompanies the publication of this book includes many of the drawings Rees removed from his European sketchbooks, as well as selected paintings and drawings related to sketchbook drawings.

Many sketchbook drawings are the basis for paintings, or other larger drawings he made for exhibition and sale. Lloyd Rees often returned to subjects which attracted him most, re-visiting favourite places and with that in mind, returning to hotels he had stayed in before.

EUROPE, 1953

The first of his European sketchbooks is a small 'Navigating Officer's Note Book' bound in yellow cloth (the AGNSW's 'Rees sketchbook no. 2'), purchased in Sydney at Swain's stationers in Pitt Street. Measuring just 11 x 16.5 centimetres it fits comfortably in one hand. Part of the binding incorporates a sleeve or holder for a pencil. Rees drew in this sketchbook in carbon pencil because he had begun to favour its soft blackness.[3]

The first drawings in sketchbook no. 2, of Singapore, are however in pencil. Singapore was one of the ports of call of the ship on which he and Marjory Rees were travelling *en route* to Europe with son Alan and niece Gwynfa Rees. On 18 January 1953, a day before arriving in Naples, he wrote enthusiastically about Singapore to Daphne Mayo, clearly optimistic about the year's travelling ahead:

"…our most exciting experience. Right outside the wharf stood Chinatown – with over 3/4ths of a million in it!! … The noise, colour & mystery of it was almost overpowering …"[4]

Lloyd and Marjory Rees left Sydney for Europe in December 1952. They spent the first ten weeks in Italy and France, followed by four months in England where they were lent a house in Harrow. Rees became ill in England, a nervous condition that had intermittently plagued him since adolescence. He visited a Harley Street psychiatrist in London, but recovered before he and Marjory resumed their travels in Europe in August 1953. They had another three months in France, Spain and Italy before returning to Australia at the end of November 1953.

The first European drawings in 'sketchbook no. 2' are of Naples and Marseilles. The Reeses had a day in Marseilles on 21 January before leaving the ship in Genoa. From Genoa they travelled by train to Rome. Alan Rees, their eighteen year old son, was responsible for their immediate travel plans. According to a letter his mother wrote to him dated 28 June 1959, when his parents next travelled to Europe, he did this very well:

"Have meant to tell you Alan of how amazed I continue to be at your organization of our Rail tour in 1953. You seem to have hit so many nails on the head, and within an hour of landing in Genoa! Congratulations, however belated."[5]

Lloyd Rees also used a slightly larger sketchbook in 1953, bought in France, measuring 13.5 x 18 centimetres and spiral bound rather than sewn (as is the 'Navigating Officer's Note Book'). The AGNSW's 'Rees sketchbook no. 3', it includes drawings of Venice and San Gimignano, and follows 'sketchbook no. 2' chronologically.

Douglas Dundas had recommended San Gimignano to Rees[6] – it became a favourite place for extended stays on each of his subsequent European visits. Of his first sight of San Gimignano in February 1953 he wrote:

"Arrived at night in a light snow fall after a strange trip in a strange small train on a branch line from the main Florence-Siena line …

Awoke to find country mantled in snow & landscape from window looked magical with qualities of stain glass window based on silver glass with russet tones of buildings & trees forming lovely patterns and masses linked together by the lines of the grape vines & the white roads weaving through everything. The old town a beautiful example of a medieval mountain town – winding streets & many archways & of course the famous towers breaking the sky line."

The Reeses stayed for two nights and a day and returned for a month in September 1953. They were met and befriended by the artist Cesare Vagarini and his wife Maria in San Gimignano and felt themselves 'at home' in the town. The Vagarinis had been in an internment camp in Australia during the second world war, having been arrested in Palestine as Italian nationals and sent to Australia.[7] Cesare Vagarini's frescoes and mosaics are in churches in San Gimignano and Palestine. In 1953 in San Gimignano Rees posed as St. Mark for one of Vagarini's works.

San Gimignano and the Tuscan landscape became a rich source of subject matter for Rees from the 1950s to the 1970s. In 1953 he made a number of paintings of San Gimignano. Each is closely related to drawings in his sketchbooks – the National Gallery of Victoria and the Art Gallery of South Australia both have paintings from Rees's visits to San Gimignano in 1953 in their respective collections; one is included in the exhibition associated with this publication.

Invariably Lloyd Rees found his subjects close to where he was staying, as he did in Australia. He rarely strayed very far from his hotel room, apart from day trips or organized bus tours to places he wanted to see. The adventure for him was in exploring subject matter close at hand, not searching for it.

The finest and most intensely realized drawings in his 'Navigating Officer's Note Book' are of Paris, for which Rees had an abiding affection since boyhood.[8] When visiting Paris for the first time with Daphne Mayo in 1923, the experience had fulfilled a long cherished desire. On 2 July 1923 he wrote to a Brisbane friend, Peter Templeton:

"How much dreaming and castle building was summed up at that moment."

Unfortunately Lloyd Rees lost most of his 1923 Paris drawings on a bus in London. His rediscovery of Paris as a subject thirty years later was therefore doubly significant to him. He again dwelt lovingly on the city's distinctive features, its architecture, streets and parks, and captured the splendour and vivacity of Paris in the closely observed drawings in the last half of his 'Navigating Officer's Note Book'.

In 1953 Lloyd and Marjory Rees stayed in a hotel on Rue de Bellechasse on the left bank of the Seine, not far from the current Musée d'Orsay. He spent most of his time drawing in and around the Île de la Cité, as did so many artists before him (and have since).[9] Notre-Dame Cathedral was a point of focus, as was nearby, Square René-Viviani and Rue Saint-Julien-le-Pauvre. The subjects he found in and around Rue Saint-Julien-le-Pauvre have barely altered in the fifty years since Rees first drew them. The haunting beauty of Saint-Séverin, partially visible at one end of the street, is a poignant contrast to the majesty of Notre-Dame at the other end, as they appear in his 'Navigating Officer's Note Book'. Rue Galande too is largely unchanged, as is the portal of Hôtel de Laffémas and the rooftops of the houses on Rue Saint-Julien-le-Pauvre seen above the trees from Square René-Viviani.

Rees discovered Square du Vert-Galant and the Pont-Neuf as subjects on this visit, and explored the area further in 1959 and 1966 when he and Marjory stayed in an ideally situated hotel on Place Dauphine overlooking the statue of Henri IV.

Also important in his 1953 'Navigating Officer's Note Book' is a study for his first painting in Chartres. He visited Chartres on 22 March 1953 with Marjory, son Alan and the Australian journalist Roland Pullen, a resident of Paris at the time.[10] Naturally his object was to see the famous cathedral in Chartres, although he did not attempt to draw it or its interior on this first visit.

In 1953 Rees took his painting materials with him to Europe, including a portable easel and paint box. He used it in Italy,

Marjory, Lloyd and Alan Rees in Venice, 1953
photograph by a waiter using Alan Rees's camera

France and England. There is a memorable photograph by Alan Rees of Lloyd Rees painting at his portable easel on the Grand Canal in Venice in 1953. Another photograph shows Rees, indistinguishable from the onlookers who besieged him when he was working out of doors in Venice, and one of him in a Paris street (blurred unfortunately) carrying a painting on a stretcher and with his painting materials secured to a baggage trolley. He bought drawing and painting materials in Europe, but it was not until March 1953 that he began to paint. In her diary Marjory Rees wrote of her husband's painting forays while they were in Europe in 1953 – for example, on 8 March 1953 in Paris:

"Lovely sunny day – decide to go to Versailles … L makes a little sketch in oil paint thus breaking the drought!!"

and on the following day:

"Lloyd goes to paint on banks of Seine. Bitterly cold."

She noted that he painted in the Tuileries on 10 March and on the banks of the Seine on 15 March and stayed indoors to paint when the weather was against it. On 19 July in England, she wrote:

"[Lloyd] has been busy preparing canvases to paint in Paris, so I expect we'll have some good paintings to bring home".

and on 27 July:

"…but expect to settle down in Italy on 15th Sept. where I expect L. will do some painting. He says the English landscape is not paintable for him, just too trim & perfect, but now that he is well again, he'll work in his beloved Paris."

Travelling in Europe also allowed Rees to search out works of art and architecture he wanted to see. As a part-time lecturer in drawing and history of art at the School of Architecture of Sydney University, what he saw was of particular benefit. In Italy in 1953 he wrote:

"We have been seeing a number of small places and most of the time have left our luggage at railway stations & gone off with the barest essentials.

At times my conscience worried me to be bringing Marjory & Alan into all these odd spots to look at frescoes (principally) and buildings and mosaics. However more than anything else I wanted to see the Art of Italy and you cant see it in a few great galleries as in France & England, but must go from town to town because naturally frescoes cannot be moved from the walls where they were painted. So we've been to a great number of places since leaving Rome. Perugia, Assisi, Arezzo, Ravenna, Florence, San Gimignano, Siena, Florence Bologna, Padua & Venice. I[t] was not nearly so formidable a programme as it reads – many of the places were only visited for half a day or even a couple of hours just to see isolated works and we were able to spend 5 days in Florence (not enough & we hope to get back later on) and a full wonderful week in Venice."

EUROPE, 1959

In 1959 Lloyd and Marjory Rees returned to many of the places they visited in 1953, at times almost re-tracing their steps. They travelled on the same ship as previously, Flotta Lauro's *Sydney*, stopping *en route* at Singapore, Colombo, Cochin (India), Massawa (Ethiopia), Port Said, Malta, Messina and Naples, before again disembarking, as they had in 1953, in Genoa. In separate letters from them both to various members of their respective families, including their son Alan and daughter-in-law Jan, can be gauged Lloyd and Marjory Rees's enjoyment on board and on excursions at various ports of call, in expectation of their impending arrival in Europe. They made arrangements in advance by post to stay at some of the same places and hotels as in 1953. Family was important to Rees's well-being and he and Marjory remained in close contact with as many of them as possible throughout their time away, just as they did at home in Australia. While they were at sea, Lloyd Rees's sister Amy died. They had visited her in Brisbane when their ship stopped there on its way to Singapore; Amy was gravely ill so her death was not unexpected. Nevertheless because she had been an important and dependable support to him at various times of his life, he felt her loss badly. They were also concerned about Alan and Jan Rees's first child, a girl Kristin, then aged three, who was injured in a fall in Sydney while Lloyd and Marjory Rees were on their way to Europe.

In their letters to family and friends the Reeses remarked on changes since their visit to Europe six years earlier. The post-war prosperity of the 1950s and 60s was evident – for them in particular, expansion of their much-loved Pensione Alboretti in Venice (with higher rates!) and that the Vagarinis finally had a home of their own in San Gimignano.

There were chance meetings with friends and acquaintances in Europe, including fellow artists from Australia – James Cook and Enid Cambridge, photographer Kerry Dundas (son of Douglas Dundas); they also met artists Stanley Spencer, Henry Moore and Arthur Fleischmann in England, and Max Papart and stained-glass specialist Gabriel Loire[11] in France. They travelled to Denmark to see a Danish couple they met in Landeck and again in Venice, and were received warmly in various places as a result of contacts made in 1953.

There are four sketchbooks that remain from the 1959 European tour. Intriguing is a school exercise book for Botany (the AGNSW's 'sketchbook no. 4'), a gift from Alan and Jan Rees. He referred to it in a letter from San Gimignano dated 28 June 1959:

> "You may be interested to know I've done 36 sketches this week. A change for me. Mostly water colour & not all small as I bought a big drawing book in Florence. Botany book being put to much use. Thanks to you both."

Unlike his two 1953 sketchbooks, Rees added watercolour to the drawings in those from 1959. The painterliness of the watercolour washes greatly enlivens their effect. The squarish format of the

Botany exercise book also suited him. Drawings in it are amongst his best and most freely expressive. The places featured in this sketchbook highlight the extent of their travels – Malta, Lake Como, Landeck, Venice, San Gimignano, Paris, Chartres, Dinard, Albi, Arezzo, Rome, Tivoli, Capri, Greece, Crete, Sicily, the Calabrian coast and Suez Canal.

It was their first visit to Greece and Crete in 1959. He wrote about it upon their return to Australia for the catalogue of the Society of Artists 'Spring exhibition' in 1960 – 'Grecian memories' illustrated with five of his sketchbook drawings, one of which, of the Acropolis, is in the AGNSW's 'Rees sketchbook no. 6':

> "Through the night we travelled up the Gulf of Corinth and through the famous Canal and at grey dawn were awakened by the noise of berthing in Piraeus – the Port of Athens. This is the moment when few can remain unmoved, for here around us lay the cradle of modern European civilization.
>
> … One ascends the Acropolis by gentle ramps and notes with gratitude that the natural stone of the hill has remained unspoiled by 'improvements'. The majestic entrance (Propylaea) is reached, still with the natural stone underfoot; and as one passes through, the Parthenon comes into view slightly elevated above the general level.
>
> My first impression was of the sheer beauty of its material, a light golden stone alive in the sunlight. Next came the sense of its lovely proportions and the balance of light and shade. Here indeed is a building in perfect repose, its lines ascend from the earth, create a shape and descend to earth again – the very expression of Greek reasonableness.
>
> … The temples are rarely placed on the highest peaks. That would destroy their scale; but rather are they placed on lesser peaks with greater ones surrounding them to remind one that the gods look down upon the works of man … Having always imagined it [the Acropolis] as the dominating feature of the landscape, I was spellbound by the majesty of its surrounding landscape, dominated by ranges and soaring peaks."

The AGNSW's 'Rees sketchbook no. 5' also has many spirited and exceptional drawings. Rees removed a number from this sketchbook (now in public and private collections) but retained most. It is spiral bound, the same kind and size as the AGNSW's 'Rees sketchbook no. 3' from 1953. There are some drawings of Werri subjects at the beginning of the sketchbook, but fifty

European drawings remain – drawings of places visited in Italy, France and Greece. Revisiting favourite places often yielded the best drawings – the statue of Henri IV from Square du Vert-Galant and their hotel on Place Dauphine in Paris, the Villa Medici and Trinità dei Monti in Rome for example. Most of the drawings remaining in the sketchbook are of San Gimignano and the Tuscan landscape. He and Marjory wrote feelingly to Stan and Min Pollard, Marjory's brother and sister-in-law, of their stay there. Marjory Rees on 21 June 1959:

> "…our room opens on to a beautiful terrace, the flat roof of the dining room below. It is very lovely; L. says it's worth coming all the way just to see this wonderful Tuscan landscape. Wheat harvest is in full swing and the summer is still early. To-day was hot at mid-day. There's a long twilight & L. is doing a pencil – or water colour – sketch before dinner at 8pm."

On 28 June 1959 Lloyd Rees to Alan and Jan Rees:

> "Am writing this on the terrace outside our room – in the gloaming! Half of Tuscany seems spread out before me and it is glorious. As a matter of fact I really think we are in one of the unique spots in Italy with this wonderful old town & its towers looming up behind & the magical landscape falling away hill beyond hill each with its villa or palace bosomed in cypress & the slopes a rhythm of vine & olive among which the farm houses nestle in their dull ochres & golden hay stacks. You must all come here some day!"

and on 3 July 1959 before leaving San Gimignano:

> "This is our last night in San Gimignano & the Vagarinis are coming here to dinner. We shall miss these wonderful evenings on our terrace. The late sun has turned the hills to gold & the perfumed landscape is very still. I think we forgot to mention the beautiful scent, like orange blossoms, which arises from the valley."

EUROPE, 1966–67

Five sketchbooks remain from Lloyd Rees's trip to Europe in 1966-67. Outstanding is the AGNSW's 'Rees sketchbook no. 11'. Pocket-sized, it is a Winsor and Newton maroon covered sketchbook with perforated tear-lines for removing drawings. Arguably it is his finest existing sketchbook. A larger version of the same kind of sketchbook, is the AGNSW's 'Rees sketchbook no. 15' used on the same European visit and including drawings of Spain and Majorca; also Genoa, Naples and Malta on their return to Australia via the Suez Canal. The remainder of 'sketchbook no. 15' has mainly drawings of Tasmania which had just experienced terrible bushfires. Lloyd and Marjory Rees visited Hobart immediately after their return from Europe, because their son Alan had just moved there to take up his appointment as Deputy Librarian at the University of Tasmania.

What is exceptional about the AGNSW's 'Rees sketchbook no. 11' however, is the quality and consistency of the drawings in it. It presents a seamless record of his travels and unquenchable enthusiasm for drawing. There is a natural ease and joy in the delineation of all of the eighty-seven drawings which remain with the sketchbook, including those he removed. He made each drawing rapidly, but not without due attention to the subject's essentials, often making several drawings in a day. Drawing what he saw was obviously what mattered most to him on his travels.

Twenty of the drawings he removed from 'sketchbook no. 11' remained in Rees's possession and are now in the Art Gallery of New South Wales collection. A handful of drawings Rees removed were sold; only four pages of the sketchbook are not accounted for. It is possible to identify the original positions of drawings removed because the paper strips or stubs with his inscribed titles, remaining in the sketchbook after removal, aid in their identification. Rees thought sufficiently highly of the drawings in this sketchbook to include fourteen in his selection of drawings for a book published by John Brackenreg's Australian Artist Editions in 1978, the first on his drawings.[12]

Using pen and black ink, carbon pencil and watercolour, each of these drawings is an evocative, fully realized, independent work of art. The texture, which a small sheet of sandpaper placed under the page creates when drawing, further animates Rees's distinctive draughtsmanship. Using sandpaper in this way when drawing, was a device he resorted to at times from the mid 1960s in order to prevent glibness. For the same reason he favoured an old fountain pen "that used to kick", especially when using the back of the nib. Drawings of the Greek Islands predominate in 'sketchbook no. 11'. Those of Mýkonos alone whet the appetite, but there are equally lively and seductive drawings of Daphní, Nauplion and Delphi, not to mention those made in Italy – namely of Florence, Venice, Bassano and Torcello. The expressive simplicity of *Mountains of Delphi*, formerly page 135 of the sketchbook, provided Rees with the basis for an exceptional larger drawing on Japanese mulberry paper, *Delphi I* 1966. The sketchbook concludes on a high note with a group of drawings of Paris, several drawn from his hotel window, again on the Place Dauphine, as in 1959. The last drawing, in carbon pencil and watercolour, is an arresting, brooding night scene featuring Pont-Neuf.

The AGNSW's 'Rees sketchbook no. 12' has many drawings of Portugal, Spain and Majorca. Lloyd and Marjory Rees spent several weeks in a small stone cottage at Fornalutx near Soller on Majorca. The Australian painter Jean Bellette, who lived near Soller with her husband Paul Haefliger, encouraged Rees to come to Majorca. Friends of hers recommended Fornalutx. While Marjory recuperated from a bad bout of influenza there, Rees drew the rugged landscape virtually on their doorstep. Coincidentally, the cottage belonged to an Australian, Len Harrop, Professor of Spanish at the University of New South Wales, known to Alan Rees. Lloyd Rees did not know him but sought out Professor Harrop soon after arrival in Majorca. In a letter to Jan and Alan Rees on 28 January 1967 Rees described the cottage as:

> "… the quaintest thing imaginable with odd corners & a sun terrace. You couldn't take a vehicle up the winding cobbled stairs which wind up the hill so wood & other heavy stores come by donkeys."

and on 10 February 1967 to Daphne Mayo, of the environment in which it was situated:

> "The landscape is like a drug it is so beautiful. Not only in details such as peasant architecture & clustering villages but in great majestic forms culminating in peaks going up to 5000 feet & all within a few miles of our door."

Two other sketchbooks Rees used on this trip, the AGNSW's 'Rees sketchbooks 13 and 14', comprise drawings he made on their travels to England and France. Béziers in Languedoc, southern France, yielded a rich vein of drawings for one of Rees's greatest later paintings, *A tribute to France* 1968–69, purchased by the Gallery shortly after it was completed in Sydney. Taking in a grand sweep of the French countryside with a river coursing through it, cultivated farmland on either side and a view to distant mountains, this painting is classic Rees – panoramic and from an elevated viewpoint, it is infused with an all pervading high-key

Lloyd Rees, *A tribute to France* 1968–69 oil on canvas, 116.9 x 132.1 cm
Art Gallery of New South Wales. Purchased 1969

summer light, an ecstatic affirmation of life and goodness. There are seven known drawings related to the painting, all but one of which are from 'sketchbooks 13 and 14'. Rees gave one of the drawings for the painting, from 'sketchbook no. 13', to the Art Gallery of New South Wales shortly after it purchased *A tribute to France*. Another from the same sketchbook was sold to the National Gallery in Canberra. When all seven drawings are considered together and shown with the painting, Rees's process, or the fundamental part drawing plays in his work, is revealed.

Rees's sketchbook drawings for *A tribute to France* are from St. Nazaire in Béziers. Clearly visible from this vantage point is an old water mill on the River Orb, Moulin Cordier, an important part of the painting's composition, though amplified by Rees in keeping with his romantic and imaginative inclinations. He and Marjory Rees spent five days in Béziers and while there also sought out the expatriate Australian painter Fred Jessup, who still lives at nearby Servian.

Rees occasionally wrote in his sketchbooks – notes about works of art seen in museums or drafts of letters. His sketchbooks also proved useful when, in 1976, he was encouraged to make soft-ground etchings for the newly formed Port Jackson Press, in Sydney. He based the first series of his etchings on drawings in his sketchbooks. Thirteen etchings, six of which were sold in a portfolio as *Memories of Europe*, resulted. Those of Majorca – *Plaza Soller, Majorca; Farm House, Majorca* and *"Our home" in Majorca*, and of Greece – *Greek Islands* and *Monastery, Corfu*, are instantly recognizable from drawings in his 1966–67 sketchbooks, notably in the AGNSW's 'Rees sketchbooks 11, 12 and 15.'

Rees and his wife also visited museums and exhibitions in 1966, as they did on all of their European trips – he noted those of Morandi and Boccioni in Venice, Manet and Bonnard in Paris and Rouault in London. They met up with Australian artists Jean Bellette and Paul Haefliger in Majorca, Brett Whiteley and art critic Robert Hughes in London, and visited the Australian sculptor Barbara Tribe in Mousehole, England. Barbara Tribe modelled Rees's bust while he and Marjory were with her.[13] He made a drawing of it in 'sketchbook no. 12'.

EUROPE, 1973

In 1973 Lloyd and Marjory Rees travelled to London to be present at the opening of an exhibition of his work at the New Grafton Gallery. It was Rees's first important solo exhibition outside Australia. John Brackenreg, long-time friend and a dealer in his work in Sydney, arranged the exhibition following the success of the Art Gallery of New South Wales's Lloyd Rees retrospective, touring nationally 1969–70 and curator Renée Free's subsequent monograph, published in 1972.

The Reeses extended their European stay in 1973 to spend time in France and Italy, especially San Gimignano, Chartres and Vézelay. Although there are only the scrappy remains of two sketchbooks from this visit, each place led to an outpouring of creative energy that almost surpassed that of longer earlier trips to Europe. Numerous exhibitions of his drawings after their travels 1973 also account for the lack of extant sketchbooks. There was no desire to keep them intact as source material, as there had been for earlier European trips. Several of the many drawings removed from his two 1973 sketchbooks have been traced, including a number of small studies of the interior of Chartres Cathedral.

The majority of his drawings and paintings of Chartres belong to Sydney University, where collectively they sum up Rees's lifelong

fascination with cathedral interiors. He described his time in Chartres Cathedral in a letter from Vézelay to his son dated 15 July 1973:

"The Chartres experience of nearly 5 days was – for me at all events – a memorable one. I spent the major part of each day inside the great building drawing & working in watercolours. Even if there's no development in oils when I get home the experience has been wonderful."

Back in Australia Rees concentrated on his Chartres, San Gimignano and Vézelay works, Chartres in particular. As Marjory Rees wrote on 26 November 1973 from their Werri holiday house on the south coast of New South Wales:

"Dad showed his 10 Cathedral drawings on which he has been spending time during the drizzly days down here – I think you would be staggered at all the work he has done on these memories of Chartres".

and on 24 January 1974 from Northwood:

"Home from Werri on 22/1 – Dad very busy there – on wet days he sat in front of the big window and completed drawings of Chartres Cathedral interior – He must have started 12 or 14 during our visit there".

The drawings of San Gimignano which resulted from their month long stay in 1973 must be counted among his most accomplished. The town of Vézelay was a new discovery for him. Its basilica and surrounding French countryside gave Rees a feast of fresh subjects resulting in at least one major painting, now in Perth at the Art Gallery of Western Australia. Unfortunately there are only a few drawings of Vézelay remaining in his two sketchbooks from 1973.

On 5 June 1973, prior to leaving for Vézelay, Rees had written:

"We grow excited at the prospect of France & staying for 2 weeks in Vezelay in Burgundy & the more we see of it (in pictures) & hear of it and its environment, the more our anticipation grows."

There is a new urgency apparent in his sketchbook drawings in 1973, reflecting a search for more immediate pictorial synthesis in paint. Rees was no longer making a detailed record from which to work later. His drawings are notational and summary. The impulse to draw and paint had become the same; he could more readily than ever before re-live and transform his experiences into drawings and paintings.

Lloyd and Marjory Rees were not without the inevitable problems of extended overseas travel in 1973. They were both in their late seventies; he was sick for some of the time and Marjory fell and injured a leg in San Gimignano, necessitating awkward bus trips to Siena for X-rays. They remained inveterate travellers however, Rees and his family returning to Paris for an exhibition of his work there in 1987, a year before he died aged 93.

George Lawrence, artist friend and Northwood neighbour, accompanied the Reeses to France and Italy in 1973. Rees and Lawrence had been painting companions often enough before as members of the 'Northwood Group'.[14] They spurred one another on to make the most of their time in Europe. As Marjory Rees wrote from San Gimignano on 4 August:

> "Dad has found yet another subject which fills him with excitement and fortunately there was a shady spot from which to work … Dad and G.L. worked like slaves during 5 days at Chartres and a fortnight at Vézelay.
>   There are some completed drawings and sketches galore from which oil paintings might develop."

and on 26 August:

> "Dad has done no oil paintings here but these 10 weeks in Europe have produced an amazing number of drawings – watercolours in various sizes – including some in small sketchbooks …"

Notes

1. Refer to exhibition catalogue *Lloyd Rees, early Brisbane drawings 1913–17* Queensland University at the Customs House, Brisbane 1995. This exhibition coincided with the Queensland Art Gallery's showing of *Lloyd Rees drawings, centenary retrospective* from the AGNSW in November-December 1995. The earliest of Rees's remaining sketchbooks comprises Brisbane subjects from 1913–14; the sketchbook was a gift to Rees from the bookbinder Wal Taylor. It is the AGNSW's 'Rees sketchbook no. 1'.

2. Rees and Mayo were engaged in the first half of 1922. He sent her an opal ring. Mayo broke off the engagement in 1925 and never married. Daphne Mayo (1895–1982) won the Queensland Wattle Day League's first travelling art scholarship in 1913. She delayed taking it up until 1919 ie. after the first world war. She studied at the Royal Academy 1920–23 where she won the Landseer Scholarship and a bronze medal in 1921, two silver medals in 1922, a gold medal for sculpture and the Edward Stott Travelling Scholarship to Rome in 1923. Refer to Judith McKay *Daphne Mayo, sculptor* exhibition catalogue, University Art Museum, University of Queensland 1981.

3. According to a letter to Norman Carter from Lloyd Rees dated 7 November 1959, Norman Carter introduced Rees to carbon pencil in the late 1940s. Refer to Norman Carter correspondence, State Library of NSW. In a taped interview on 18 August 1978, concerning works of his in the collection of the National Gallery, Canberra, Rees told James Gleeson: "Carbon pencil was very much adopted by me, because I found that you could draw a line and then when you put the wash over, every bit of loose carbon became melted. It gave a slight greyness to your wash, but it left a line so clear that I remember even Wallace Thornton thought they were pen drawings once, you see …" (transcript of tape courtesy of Alan and Jancis Rees, Hobart and National Gallery, Canberra).

4. Correspondence between Lloyd Rees and Daphne Mayo is in the Fryer Library, University of Queensland, Brisbane. All quotations are given as written, irrespective of inconsistencies of spelling, punctuation etc.

5. Correspondence between Lloyd and Marjory Rees and their family, excerpts from Marjory Rees's diary and other unpublished writings by Lloyd Rees quoted and referred to, are courtesy of Alan and Jancis Rees, Hobart.

6. Douglas Dundas (1900–81) painted San Gimignano with distinction since first discovering it for himself in 1928 on his European travels as a NSW Travelling Scholarship holder, and encouraged other artists and his students to go there. Dundas was a friend to Rees, a fellow painter, and at various times a trustee of the Art Gallery of New South Wales, President of the Society of Artists and Head of the National Art School, Sydney. As he wrote in *Art and Australia* (volume 7, no. 2, September 1969, p. 130) about Rees's work:
"The Tuscan hill town of San Gimignano is dearer to his heart, for there, as I know from experience, one is close to the earth. The stern square towers brood over the city or, alternatively, from the slopes below, are seen as golden shafts piercing a cobalt sky. The olive groves and vinèyards come right up to the ancient walls and, from the terrace of Lionello's Pensione Bel Soggiorno, Lloyd Rees draws subject-matter from the great sweep of landscape dotted with farmhouses that leads down to the Val d'Elsa and the sun-soaked hills beyond. And it may well be that, despite their very different history, the stones of San Gimignano have a close affinity in the mind of Lloyd Rees with the Sydney sandstone he has portrayed with such insight throughout his life."

7. Refer to exhibition catalogue *The work of the Italian painter Cesare Vagarini at POW Camp 3, Tatura, during World War II* Benalla Art Gallery 1999. There is a drawing and a painting by Cesare Vagarini in the Art Gallery of New South Wales collection.

8. As a young man Rees liked to re-invent Brisbane in drawings, according to what he knew of Paris from books. One such book he had owned since 1913, is by S.L. Bensusan *Souvenir of Paris* London: Jack, undated.

9. It is interesting to compare Rees's sketchbook drawings of Paris, along the Seine between Notre-Dame and Pont Neuf, with the work of Jongkind, Pissarro, Signac, Matisse, Marquet, Picasso, De Stael and others, eg. in the catalogue to a recent exhibition *Paris, sous le ciel de la peinture* held at Salle Saint-Jean, Hôtel de Ville de Paris 14 September – 17 December 2000.

10. Roland Pullen lived in Rue de Fürstenberg, best known as the street on which Eugene Delacroix lived. Delacroix's house is now a museum. The Reeses stayed in Roland Pullen's apartment on Rue de Fürstenberg throughout August 1953. There is a drawing by him of Rue de Fürstenberg in the AGNSW's 'Rees sketchbook no. 2.'

11. Rees wrote about meeting Loire – 'Gabriel Loire maître-verrier a Chartres' – in the catalogue for the Society of Artists annual 'Drawings and prints' exhibition at David Jones' Art Gallery, Sydney 4–13 May 1960.

12. *Lloyd Rees drawings* Sydney: Australian Artist Editions 1978. Foreword by Joseph Burke, edited and with an introduction by Lou Klepac.

13. Patricia R. McDonald *Barbara Tribe, sculptor* Sydney: Craftsman House, 2000 pp. 43, 107 (Plate 28). A bronze of the bust is in the collection of the Art Gallery of New South Wales.

14. The Northwood Group was a loose association of friends who enjoyed one another's company, had similar values as artists and met to draw the figure or paint out-of-doors. Roland Wakelin and John Santry were also well known members of the group.

Explanatory notes

Nineteen sketchbooks by Lloyd Rees are extant, all of which are in the collection of the Art Gallery of New South Wales, a gift from Alan and Jancis Rees, the artist's son and daughter-in-law. Thirteen of these were used by Rees on his four extended visits to Europe in 1953, 1959, 1966–67 and 1973. The drawings illustrated in this publication are selected from his 'European' sketchbooks.

There are almost 700 drawings altogether in Rees's extant sketchbooks; he removed a number for sale and exhibition, but some of those removed he retained – most of these are also in the Art Gallery of New South Wales collection – identified as 'from' a particular sketchbook. On his later European visits Rees used a piece of sandpaper or emery paper under the sketchbook page on which he was drawing, which accounts for the textured quality of some of his drawings. Measurements are given in centimetres height before width, and only the artist's inscriptions are given unless stated otherwise. Wherever possible drawings are reproduced actual size.

The artist's inscribed titles for drawings, or place names, often appear on facing pages, i.e. the verso of previous drawings in sketchbooks. It is therefore important to ascertain page order in respect to drawings removed from sketchbooks, because an inscription on verso refers to the drawing which follows.

Quotations from the artist or his wife Marjory Rees, accompanying the commentary to selected drawings, are given as they are written, irrespective of inconsistencies of spelling, punctuation etc.

A number of guide books were useful in the identification of places and buildings, e.g. the *Eyewitness Travel Guides* published by Dorling Kindersley, London between 1993 and 1997; *Michelin* guides and numerous guide books of individual towns. So too the Pelican History of Art series edited by Nikolaus Pevsner: *Early Christian and Byzantine architecture, Greek architecture, Etruscan and Roman Architecture,* and *Art and architecture of the eighteenth century in France,* published by Penguin between 1957 and 1972; *The Times atlas of the world* London: Harper Collins 1994; John James, *Chartres, the masons who built a legend* London: Routledge and Kegan Paul 1982; *Atget Paris* Paris: Hazan 1992; *Marville Paris* Paris: Hazan 1994; the Könemann Art and Architecture books on *Venice, Florence* and *Andalusia* published in 1999; and Michel Poisson, *Paris buildings and monuments* New York: Abrams 1999.

Abbreviations

Free *Rees* 1972:
Renée Free, *Lloyd Rees* Melbourne: Lansdowne 1972

Rees drawings 1978:
Lou Klepac, *Lloyd Rees drawings* Sydney: Australian Artist Editions 1978

Later works 1983:
Renée Free and Lloyd Rees, *Lloyd Rees, the later works* Sydney: Craftsman's Press 1983 (re-issued as *Lloyd Rees: the last twenty years* Sydney: Craftsman House, 1990)

Rees etchings and lithographs 1986:
Hendrik Kolenberg, *Lloyd Rees, etchings and lithographs; a catalogue raisonné* Sydney: The Beagle Press, 1986

Artist remembers 1987:
Renée Free and Lloyd Rees, *Lloyd Rees, an artist remembers* Sydney: Craftsman House, 1987

Rees drawings AGNSW 1995:
Hendrik Kolenberg, *Lloyd Rees drawings, centenary retrospective* Sydney: Art Gallery of New South Wales 1995

Australian drawings AGNSW 1997:
Hendrik Kolenberg, *Australian drawings from the Gallery's collection* Sydney: Art Gallery of New South Wales, 1997

AGNSW:
Art Gallery of New South Wales, Sydney

THE DRAWINGS

1953

Lloyd and Marjory Rees, accompanied by their son Alan and niece Gwynfa Rees, left Sydney by ship for Europe on Flotta Lauro's *Sydney* on 16 December 1952. They spent ten weeks in Italy and France followed by four months in Britain and another three months in France, Spain and Italy before boarding the *Orcades* in Naples on 2 November 1953, for their return to Australia.

> "On that first trip I was, I suppose, working like a tourist: that is, a tourist without a camera but with sketchbooks, quite small, pocket size."
> (*Artist remembers* 1987 p. 69)

1 *Naples* 1953

in sketchbook no. 2, p. 17; pencil, carbon pencil 10.1 x 16
inscribed, dated in pencil 'NAPOLI 18.1.53' lower left
illustrated: Free *Rees* 1972, p. 62 (41; D 199)

Naples was the first European port of call for Lloyd and Marjory Rees. They stayed
two days. This is one of two drawings of Naples in sketchbook no. 2.

2 *Pavement café, Marseilles* 1953
in sketchbook no. 2, p. 13; pencil, carbon pencil, grey wash 10.1 x 16
inscribed in pencil 'HOTEL IN FRANCE' on facing p. 12 lower right

Marseilles was their second European port of call before disembarkation at Genoa. They were there on 21 January 1953. In her diary Marjory Rees wrote:

> "Lloyd Gwynfa & I have a French meal in cafe … Then we walk up Cannebière which widens – trees (leafless) – find little square & rest for a while".

Gwynfa is Lloyd Rees's niece, the daughter of his brother, Vernon. She was 21 years of age at the time. She left from Genoa, soon after their arrival in Italy, for a working holiday in England.

3 *Landscape, Arezzo* 1953
in sketchbook no. 2, p. 29; pencil, carbon pencil 10.1 x 15.9
inscribed in pencil 'AREZZO' lower right

Lloyd and Marjory Rees were in Arezzo on 4 February 1953. According to Marjory Rees's diary:

> "… train to Arezzo … see beautiful church … the Duomo is closed – & we walk into a park with huge grp. of statues and a wall overlooking magnificent scenery in every direction."

4 *Duomo, Siena* 1953
in sketchbook no. 2, p. 37
pencil, carbon pencil 10.1 x 16.1
inscribed twice in pencil 'SIENA / SIENA' lower left

Siena's Duomo, constructed between 1136 and 1382, is one of Italy's finest cathedrals and dominates the skyline. Lloyd and Marjory Rees arrived in Siena on 11 February 1953 and stayed until the 13th. As Lloyd Rees wrote at the time:

> "Arrived on a wet day – snow on the hills. Lost in the maze of streets but eventually found the majestic Piazza del Campo with its soaring tower – The Mangia – one of the finest in all Italy. Market day in the Piazza, a gay sight in spite of rain. Sudden squall made us take shelter in courtyard of Palazzo Pubblico – austere & impressive. Short visit to Cathedral but too dark to see anything. Cold & hungry & set out to find a restaurant – a harder task than in any city thus far but a sign on a wall led us down a winding street where we found a restaurant (not the one advertised) but which turned out to be the most fascinating & the cheapest we'd found in Italy."

5 *Chartres* 1953

in sketchbook no. 2, p. 61
pencil, carbon pencil 10.1 x 16.1
reference: Free *Rees* 1972 (D 198)

This drawing is the basis for the painting *Chartres* 1953 (Free *Rees* 1972, p. 73, Plate 17, 0 155). Lloyd and Marjory Rees, accompanied by Alan, their son, made their first visit to Chartres on 22 March 1953. It was a day trip during the month of March when they were in Paris, staying in the Hotel de Saumur on Rue de Bellechasse. Roland Pullen, an Australian journalist who lived in Paris, acted as their guide. According to Marjory Rees's diary:

> "Chartres – Lovely day … Two uneven spires of Cathedral – we approach about 11am. Service is on … Marvellous glass windows … Cathedral is beautiful outside too. At rear is little park. L. begins to paint …"

As Lloyd Rees told AGNSW curator Renée Free later:

> "Of course, I'd heard of this building and read of it quite frequently, but had no understanding really of the impact it would make. Externally, of course, it is very simple … when we had spent hours in the building itself, we went round to the rear of the structure and I did a painting. I did not attempt to draw or paint the building." (Undated transcript of tape, AGNSW files.)

6 *Arc de Triomphe du Carrousel, Paris* 1953
in sketchbook no. 2, p. 133
carbon pencil, grey wash 10.1 x 16
inscribed in carbon pencil 'COURT OF LOUVRE' on facing p. 132 lower right

A prominent landmark for visitors to the Louvre, the Arc de Triomphe du
Carrousel is situated alongside Place du Carrousel leading toward the Jardin des
Tuileries.

7 *Quai des Grands Augustins, Paris* 1953
in sketchbook no. 2, p. 103
pencil, carbon pencil 10.1 x 16

In this drawing Rees has included the distinctive bookstalls (les bouquinistes) on the banks of the Seine which offer passers-by second hand books and prints. The embankment of Quai des Grands-Augustins directs our attention to the Pont-Neuf. The Pavillon Denon of the Louvre is in the distance. Other drawings of the subject are on pp. 91 and 93 of sketchbook no. 2.

8 *Square du Vert-Galant, Île de la Cité, Paris* 1953
in sketchbook no. 2, p. 141
carbon pencil, grey wash 10.1 x 15.8

The Seine, Pont-Neuf and Square du Vert-Galant, from Quai de Conti. Square du Vert-Galant is on the extremity of Île de la Cité which the Pont-Neuf bridges. Above it on the Pont-Neuf is the statue of Henri IV on horseback. Le Vert Galant refers to Henri IV (Henri de Navarre), who was described as "Vert galant" (or a womaniser) by many in his time, including his friend and supporter, the philosopher Montaigne.

9 *The Pont-Neuf from the embankment, Quai de Conti, Paris* 1953
in sketchbook no. 2, p. 95
carbon pencil, grey wash 10.1 x 16

In this drawing Rees has incorporated the curving wall near the steps to the Pont des Arts from the embankment of Quai de Conti and formed his composition around it and Pont-Neuf. The spire of Sainte-Chapelle is clearly visible in the middle distance, as is the nearer of the two towers of the Chambres Correctionnelles of the Palais de Justice.

10 *Boulevard du Palais, Paris* 1953

in sketchbook no. 2, p. 119
carbon pencil, grey wash 10.1 x 16

To the left in this drawing is the tower of the Chambres Correctionnelles of the Palais de Justice set at 45° to the corner of Quai des Orfèvres and Boulevard du Palais. To the right is the great dome of the Tribunal de Commerce; Tour Saint-Jacques is in the distance.

11 *Pont au Double, Paris* 1953
in sketchbook no. 2, p. 123
carbon pencil, grey wash 10.1 x 16

The Pont au Double from Quai de Montebello with the Treasury of the Notre-
Dame on the left and the clock tower of the Gare de Lyon in the distance.
Pont au Double is the link across the Seine between Notre-Dame, Square René-
Viviani and Rue Saint-Julien-le-Pauvre, the focus of so much of Rees's attention
in Paris in 1953.

12 *Île de la Cité, Paris* 1953

in sketchbook no. 2, p. 135
carbon pencil, grey wash 10.1 x 16
inscribed in carbon pencil 'THE CITE' on facing p. 134 lower right

This is the most popular aspect of the centre of Paris showing Notre-Dame and Pont-Neuf. Rees first drew Notre-Dame and other Paris landmarks in 1913, referring to photographs in his copy of S.L. Bensusan's *Souvenir of Paris*. He first visited Paris with the Brisbane sculptor, Daphne Mayo in 1923.

13 *Petit Pont and Pont Saint-Michel from Notre-Dame, Paris* 1953

in sketchbook no. 2, p. 145
carbon pencil, grey wash 10.1 x 16

Rees drew this from the parapet of Notre-Dame, a faithful rendition of the view of Petit Pont and Pont Saint-Michel below. It is Rees's grasp of great space, his ability to select the essentials and render them convincingly on a small scale, which is impressive in this drawing.

14 *Notre-Dame from Rue Saint-Julien-le-Pauvre, Paris* 1953

in sketchbook no. 2, p. 139
carbon pencil, grey wash 10.1 x 15.8
inscribed in carbon pencil and pen and blue-black ink 'RUE SAINT JULIEN/LE PAUVE PAUVRE / PAURVE'
on facing p. 138 lower right
illustrated: 'Annual report' Art Gallery of New South Wales 1995 p. 31; *Australian drawings* AGNSW 1997 p. 16

Lovingly drawn, this is one of the finest drawings in sketchbook no. 2. It emphasizes
Rees's attachment to Paris and its landmarks, especially its most famous cathedral.

15 *From Square René-Viviani, Paris* 1953

in sketchbook no. 2, p. 117
carbon pencil, black ink wash 10.1 x 16
inscribed in carbon pencil 'SQUARE RENE VIVIANI' on facing p. 116 lower right

Square René-Viviani is the church close for Saint-Julien-le-Pauvre. There is an uninterrupted view of Notre-Dame nearby. In this drawing Rees portrays the houses on the Rue Saint-Julien-le-Pauvre visible above the trees in this park.

16 *The portal of Hôtel de Laffémas, Rue Saint-Julien-le-Pauvre, Paris* 1953

in sketchbook no. 2, p. 127
carbon pencil, grey wash 10.1 x 16
inscribed in carbon pencil 'RUE SAINT JULIEN LE PAUVRE' on facing p. 126 lower right

The portal to the right of the drawing is directly opposite Saint-Julien-le-Pauvre.

17 *Rue Galande, Paris* 1953

in sketchbook no. 2, p. 131
carbon pencil, grey wash 10.1 x 15.9
inscribed in carbon pencil 'RUE GALANCE' on facing p. 130 lower right

Little has altered in Rue Galande in the fifty years since this drawing was made.
The café is now a Chinese restaurant and the pavement stalls at the front of the
shop next to it have gone. The ghostly presence of Saint-Séverin appears at the end
of the street to the right in this drawing.

37

18 *Boat builder's house, Venice* 1953

in sketchbook no. 3, p. 9
carbon pencil 13.4 x 18
inscribed in carbon pencil 'VENICE – BOAT BUILDERS HOUSE' lower left

This is the gondola yard on the Rio San Trovaso, one of very few remaining in
Venice. It is not far from the Pensione Alboretti at which Lloyd, Marjory and Alan
Rees stayed. They were in Venice 15–22 February 1953, and again from 10–17
September, when this drawing was made.

19 *Rio di San Barnaba and Ponte dei Pugni, Venice* 1953

in sketchbook no. 3, p. 13
carbon pencil 13.4 x 18
inscribed in carbon pencil 'VENICE' lower left

20 *Pensione Alboretti, Venice* 1953

in sketchbook no. 3, p. 15
carbon pencil, grey wash 13.4 x 18

Lloyd and Marjory Rees stayed at the Pensione Alboretti in 1953 and on all their
subsequent visits to Venice. Alan Rees, their son, was responsible for finding it. It is
well situated on the Rio Terrà Antonio Foscarini, adjacent to the Accademia
Galleries. The street leads to the Grand Canal with a view of San Vitale on the
opposite bank. This drawing is the basis for a painting of the same subject, refer to
Free *Rees* 1972 (O 168) and *Artist remembers* 1987 pp. 68–70 (23).

21 *Santa Maria della Salute on the Grand Canal, Venice* 1953
in sketchbook no. 3, p. 19
carbon pencil 13.4 x 18

There is a painting by Lloyd Rees of this subject, which he completed in Venice.
Alan Rees photographed his father painting it in 1953 (see p. 4). In his
commentary to this painting in *Artist remembers* 1987, p. 73, Lloyd Rees compares
the pearly wintry light of Venice with that of Sydney.

22 *San Gimignano* 1953

in sketchbook no. 3, p. 25
carbon pencil, grey wash 13.4 x 18

Lloyd and Marjory Rees first visited San Gimignano 9–11
February 1953, returning for a month between 21 September and
21 October of the same year. In San Gimignano they were met
and befriended by the artist Cesare Vagarini and his wife Maria.
The Vagarinis had been interned at Tatura, a POW camp in New
South Wales during the war. According to Marjory Rees's diary

for 20 October 1953, the day before they left:

> "L. poses in cafe for V. to draw his head – Saint Mark – for
> mosaic for church in Palestine …"

This drawing, from their stay in San Gimignano in September and
October 1953, is the basis for a painting in the collection of the
Art Gallery of South Australia (Free *Rees* 1972 p. 75, plate 19,
0 166). There is also a larger drawing of the same subject, see *Rees
drawings* AGNSW 1995 (71).

23 *Tuscan landscape, San Gimignano* 1953
in sketchbook no. 3, p. 47
carbon pencil, grey wash 13.4 x 18

San Gimignano and the landscape around it became a major
preoccupation for Rees following his first visit in 1953. Another
version of this scene is in sketchbook no. 5, 1959, p. 59 and a
larger version of it, from their 1959 trip to Europe, is in the
AGNSW collection – *Tuscan drawing* 1959 (DA38.1963) included
in *Rees drawings* AGNSW 1995 (72).

To her mother, Marjory Rees wrote from San Gimignano on 22
September 1953:

> "We got here at lunch time yest … Since we were here in Feb.
> they have glassed in a very wide verandah and extended the
> dining room. These 3 walls of glass (fitted with venetian
> blinds) overlook a most wonderful view – Lloyd needn't stir a
> step for subject matter. The grey-green of the olive trees is
> lovely and the vineyards are loaded with grapes."

24 *The towers of San Gimignano* 1953

in sketchbook no. 3, p. 51
carbon pencil, grey wash 13.4 x 18

San Gimignano is renowned for its towers. The tallest tower in this drawing is the
Torre Rognosa. It was erected in the thirteenth century and was a prison until 1407
before being transformed into a clocktower. Just visible to its left is the tallest
tower in San Gimignano, the distinctive Torre Grossa; the twin towers of the
Paltoni-Salvacci Palace are to its right and to its far left is the Torre Diavolo.

25 *Landscape, San Gimignano* 1953

in sketchbook no. 3, p. 55
carbon pencil, grey wash 13.4 x 18
illustrated: *Australian drawings* AGNSW 1997 p. 16 and p. 56 (45)

This drawing is from the terrace of the Albergo 'Bel Soggiorno', San Gimignano:

> "We stayed at the 'Bel Soggiorno' five times, twice in 1953 and again in
> subsequent visits in 1959, '67 and '73. In planning our European visit we wrote
> to the proprietor asking if we could have a room opening onto the terrace.
> From that terrace I did most of my painting in oils and quite large drawings in
> both pen and carbon, often with watercolour-wash added …" (*Artist remembers*
> 1987 p. 75)

26 *Villa Medici, Rome* 1953
in sketchbook no. 3, p. 59
carbon pencil, grey wash 13.4 x 18

Lloyd and Marjory Rees visited Rome twice in 1953. This drawing
was made between 21 and 26 October, the second visit. Rees had
not been to Rome since 1924 when he accompanied Daphne
Mayo there and became entranced with the architecture, including
the Villa Medici. The Villa Medici is a sixteenth-century palace
near the top of the Spanish Steps in Rome, in the design of which
Michelangelo is believed to have been involved. Begun for
Cardinal Giovanni Ricci in about 1540, it was enlarged and

embellished by Cardinal Ferdinando dei Medici in the 1570s. In
1801 the French government under Napoleon acquired the Villa
Medici as its Academy in Rome, with the painter Horace Vernet as
the first Director; Ingres followed in the 1830s and 1840s.
Fragonard and Boucher studied there, as did the composers Berlioz
and Debussy. Best known of twentieth century Directors was the
painter Balthus in the 1940s and 1950s, when this drawing was
made.

There are a number of drawings by Rees of the Villa Medici
following his 1924 visit to Rome. Refer to *Rees drawings* AGNSW
1995 (27).

27 *Trinità dei Monti, Rome* 1953
in sketchbook no. 3, p. 61
carbon pencil, grey wash 13.4 x 18

Lloyd and Marjory Rees stayed at Pensione Frey in Rome in both 1953 and 1959,
just as he had in 1924. Situated on Via Liguria it is near Trinità dei Monti and Villa
Medici. Trinità dei Monti, from the sixteenth century, is at the top of the Spanish
Steps with spectacular views of Rome. Other drawings of this church are in
sketchbook no. 4, 1959, p. 51 and sketchbook no. 5, 1959, p. 93.

28 *Castel Nuovo, Museo Nazionale di San Martino, Naples* 1953
in sketchbook no. 3, p. 71
carbon pencil, grey wash 13.4 x 18

Lloyd and Marjory Rees stayed in Naples between 26 October and 2 November
1953, just prior to returning to Australia by ship. This view of Naples is the subject
of several drawings by Rees, including sketchbook no. 2, 1953, p. 15 and
sketchbook no. 13, 1967 pp. 13 and 15.

1959

Lloyd and Marjory Rees left Sydney for Europe aboard Flotta Lauro's *Sydney* in April 1959. They travelled in Italy and France with trips to Austria, Switzerland, Holland and Denmark. In August and September they were in England and Scotland, then returned to France and Italy before travelling to the Greek Islands and Sicily. Their return voyage to Australia left from Messina on 19 December 1959.

29 *Rio San Trovaso, Venice* 1959

in sketchbook no. 4, p. 89
carbon pencil, watercolour 17.4 x 22.7
inscribed in black felt pen 'VENICE', in pen and black ink 'SUEZ' deleted, on facing p. 88
lower left; there is a part-impression in mirror-image of the inscribed title 'VENICE' from
original facing page, upper left (Rees removed this drawing from near the front of the
sketchbook and stuck it to the top edge of p. 91)

Lloyd and Marjory Rees visited Venice between 3 and 12 June
1959 and stayed again at the Pensione Alboretti as in 1953. Rio
San Trovaso connects Canale della Giudecca and the Grand Canal
and is near the Rio Terrà Antonio Foscarini on which the Pensione
Alboretti is situated. San Vitale which features in a number of his
drawings appears behind the bridge to the left in this drawing.

30 *Venice* 1959
in sketchbook no. 4, p. 13
carbon pencil, watercolour 17.4 x 22.7
inscribed in pen and black ink 'VENICE' on facing p. 12 lower left; there is a part-impression in mirror-image of
the inscribed title from facing p. 12 upper left

31 *Towers, San Gimignano* 1959

in sketchbook no. 4, p. 25; carbon pencil, pen and black ink, wash 17.5 x 22.8
inscribed in pen and black ink 'TOWERS, SAN GIMIGNANO' on facing p. 24 lower left

Lloyd and Marjory Rees were in San Gimignano for the third time from 19 June to 4 July 1959.
Torre Rognosa features in this drawing as it does in sketchbook no. 3, 1953, p. 51.

32 *Tuscan farmhouse, San Gimignano* 1959
in sketchbook no. 5, p. 43
carbon pencil, watercolour 13.4 x 17.9
inscribed in pen and black ink 'TUSCANY' on facing p. 42 lower right

This and the following drawing (which was removed from this sketchbook) are of
the same farmhouse in the landscape outside the city walls of San Gimignano.

33 *Tuscan farmhouse, San Gimignano* 1959

from sketchbook no. 5, between pp. 48 and 49 (i)
carbon pencil, watercolour 13.4 x 17.5, left serrated edge trimmed
inscribed in pen and black ink 'TOWERS / SAN GIMIGNANO' on verso referring to the drawing which would
follow it in the sketchbook
illustrated: *Rees drawings* 1978 p. 48 (38) as 'Tuscan farmhouse, Italy'

34 *Towers, San Gimignano* 1959

from sketchbook no. 5, between pp. 48 and 49 (ii)
carbon pencil, watercolour 13.4 x 17.5, left serrated edge trimmed
inscribed in pen and black ink 'TUSCAN VILLA' on verso referring to the drawing which would follow it in the
sketchbook
illustrated: Free *Rees* 1972 p. 122 (D 202)

35 *Tuscan landscape, San Gimignano* 1959

in sketchbook no. 5, p. 59
carbon pencil, watercolour 13.4 x 17.9
inscribed in pen and black ink 'TUSCANY' on facing p. 58 lower right

An earlier version of the same subject is in sketchbook no. 3, 1953, p. 47.

36 *Sant' Agostino, San Gimignano* 1959

from sketchbook no. 5, between pp. 60 and 61
carbon pencil, watercolour 13.4 x 17.5, left serrated edge trimmed
inscribed in pen and black ink 'LANDSCAPE / FROM / SAN GIMIGNANO' on verso referring to the drawing
which would follow it in the sketchbook
illustrated: *Rees drawings* 1978 p. 46 (36) as 'The tower, San Gimignano, Italy'

Sant' Agostino is a thirteenth century monastic Gothic church built entirely of
brick. In this drawing Rees has concentrated on the entrance through the old city
wall, on the end wall of the church with its circular window and on the bell tower.
According to Marjory Rees's diary, they first visited Sant' Agostino on 10 February
1953. Maria Vagarini took them there to show them the frescoes that she and her
husband Cesare Vagarini had spent ten years restoring.

37 *Farmhouse on the road to San Gimignano* 1959

in sketchbook no. 5, p. 63
carbon pencil, watercolour 13.4 x 18
inscribed in pen and black ink 'THE ROAD TO / SAN GIMIGNANO' on facing p. 62 lower right (the
inscription on facing p. 62 does not refer to this drawing because at least two pages have been removed between
pages 62 and 63)
illustrated: *Australian drawings* AGNSW 1997, p. 16

38 *Torre del Mangia, Siena* 1959
in sketchbook no. 5, p. 61
carbon pencil, watercolour 13.4 x 18

The Torre del Mangia is the bell tower of Siena's town hall, the Palazzo Pubblico.
At 102 metres it is one of the highest medieval towers built in Italy.

On their visit to Siena on 2 July 1959 Lloyd and Marjory Rees attended the famous
Palio festival, which Lloyd Rees described in enthusiastic detail in a letter to his son
Alan, who had been with them in Siena in 1953. The Palio is held in the Piazza del
Campo in front of the Palazzo Pubblico.

39 *Institut de France, Paris* 1959
in sketchbook no. 4, p. 33
carbon pencil, watercolour 17.5 x 22.7

Lloyd and Marjory Rees were in Paris 7–31 July 1959 on their third visit there together and stayed at the City Hotel, 29 Place Dauphine. They could not have been better or more centrally situated. Place Dauphine is a quiet sheltered close which opens onto the busy road across the Pont-Neuf. They could see the Institut de France from their hotel window, as well as the statue of Henri IV and across the Seine, the Louvre in the distance. All around are subjects which have attracted artists prior to Rees (and since) – Monet, Renoir, Bonnard, Matisse, Marquet and Picasso. Camille Pissarro lived at 28 Place Dauphine for three years from November 1900 and painted in and around the area extensively.

40 *Grand Palais and Petit Palais, Paris* 1959

in sketchbook no. 5, p. 71
carbon pencil, watercolour 13.4 x 18
inscribed in pen and black ink 'PARIS' on facing p. 70 lower right

Both palaces are on the Avenue Winston-Churchill and are venues for major
exhibitions. Lloyd Rees made this drawing from the Cours la Reine near Avenue
Dutuit. In the foreground is a Citroën 'Goddess'.

41 *Henri IV, Île de la Cité, Paris* 1959

in sketchbook no. 5, p. 73
carbon pencil, watercolour 13.4 x 18
inscribed in pen and black ink 'PARIS' on facing p. 72 lower right

Rees made this drawing from the Square du Vert-Galant. Visible is
the Statue of Henri IV on Pont-Neuf and the building in which
the City Hotel was situated on Place Dauphine. As Marjory Rees
wrote in a letter on 19 July 1959:

"from our window we can read the inscription on the statue of
Henrici Magni horseman in the middle of the Pont-Neuf."

There is a painting by Picasso in the Musée Picasso of the same
subject, *Le Vert-Galant*, dated 25 June 1943 – refer to exhibition
catalogue *Paris, sous le ciel de la peinture* Hôtel de Ville de Paris
2000 pp. 194–195.

42 *Saint-Sernin, Toulouse* 1959

in sketchbook no. 5, p. 83
carbon pencil, watercolour 13.4 x 18
inscribed in pen and black ink 'ST. SURNIN / TOULOUSE' on facing p. 82 lower right

The beginnings of Basilique Saint-Sernin reach back almost a thousand years. It was finished in the 14th century and constructed of red brick and white stone. It is the biggest Romanesque church in Western Europe. Lloyd and Marjory Rees were in Toulouse for five days and nights from 21 October 1959.

43 *Pont du Gard, Nîmes* 1959

in sketchbook no. 4, p. 73
carbon pencil, watercolour 17.5 x 22.7
inscribed in black felt pen 'PONT de GARDE' on facing p. 72 lower centre and in pen
and black ink 'NEAR ATHENS' deleted lower left (Rees removed this drawing from the
sketchbook and stuck it to the back of p. 72)

Lloyd and Marjory Rees visited the aqueduct when they were in
Nîmes on 28 October 1959.

According to a letter by Lloyd Rees to his son and daughter-in-law
on 1 November 1959:

"… On way back to Nîmes we had 3 hours at Pont du Garde,
that most wonderful of Roman viaducts – spanning a gorge.
Doubt if there is any more imposing Roman relic – & it still
carries water!"

44 *Farmhouse, Vence* 1959
in sketchbook no. 5, p. 89
carbon pencil, watercolour 13.3 x 18
inscribed in pen and black ink 'VENCE / FRANCE' on facing p. 88 lower right

Lloyd and Marjory Rees left Nîmes for Nice on 29 October. From Nice they visited
Vence and Monte Carlo and reached Genoa on 31 October. From Genoa they
travelled to Florence, then to Arezzo and Rome.

In all likelihood the drawing of Vence in the collection of Newman College,
University of Melbourne, was originally between pp. 88 and 89. On its verso is
inscribed 'Vence' referring to this drawing.

45 *Arezzo* 1959

in sketchbook no. 4, p. 47
carbon pencil, watercolour 17.5 x 22.7
there is a part-impression of a mirror-image of the inscribed title 'AREZZO' from the
original facing page (now missing) upper left
illustrated: *Australian drawings* AGNSW 1997 p. 16

Lloyd and Marjory Rees were in Arezzo 5–6 November. As Rees
wrote from Rome to his son and daughter-in-law on 8 November:

"Stayed at a beauty [a hotel] at Arezzo on the way here, right
alongside the church with the famous Piero della Francesco
frescoes & discovered a fascinating restaurant in a crypt right
near the church also. Went up on the terrace near cathedral &
sketched …"

46 *Trinità dei Monti, Rome* 1959

in sketchbook no. 5, p. 93
carbon pencil, watercolour 13.5 x 18
inscribed in pen and black ink 'ROME' on facing p. 92 lower right

Lloyd and Marjory Rees were in Rome between 6 and 23 November 1959 and again stayed at Pensione Frey as in 1924 and 1953. As he wrote to Alan and Jan Rees on 8 November 1959:

"Well here we are back in the old spot. I suppose we are conservative but it's a relief to come to a known spot & not have to adjust oneself".

And again on 24 November 1959:

"We left Pension Frey with regret. It was the most 'home like' place we've stayed in."

On the same visit Rees drew this church in sketchbook no. 4, 1959, p. 49. It also appears in sketchbook no. 3, 1953, p. 61.

47 *The temple, Tivoli* 1959

in sketchbook no. 5, p. 97
carbon pencil, watercolour 13.4 x 18
inscribed in pen and black ink 'THE TEMPLE / TIVOLI' on facing p. 96 lower right

48 *Capri* 1959

in sketchbook no. 5, p. 107
carbon pencil, watercolour 13.4 x 18
inscribed in pen and black ink 'CARRI' on facing p. 106 lower right

This drawing was made on the day trip Lloyd and Marjory Rees took to Capri from
Naples on 25 November 1959.

49 *Candia, Crete* 1959

in sketchbook no. 5, p. 27
carbon pencil, watercolour 13.4 x 18
inscribed in pen and black ink 'TITLES / FACING / DRAWINGS' on facing p. 26 upper left, 'CANDIA / CRETE' and in pencil 'CANDIA' lower right

Lloyd and Marjory Rees were in Crete on 28 and 29 November 1959 and again on 4 October 1966. In a letter to Alan and Jan Rees from Athens on 4 December 1959 Lloyd Rees wrote:

"In the meantime we have been to Crete – it was the terminus of boat trip from Brindisi. There we saw the great ruins of Palace of Knossos & sculptural & painting relics of a civilization dating back to about 2000 BC."

Candia is an earlier name for Irákleio as it is called now. The Venetians named it Candia in the 13th century.

50 *Crete* 1959

in sketchbook no. 6, p. 3
carbon pencil, watercolour 14.9 x 20.7
inscribed in pen and black ink 'GREECE /(CRETE)' on facing p. 2 lower right

51 *The Propylaia, Athens* 1959

in sketchbook no. 6, p. 5
carbon pencil, watercolour 14.8 x 20.6
inscribed in pen and black ink 'ATHENS' on facing p. 4 lower right
illustrated: Free *Rees* 1972 p. 77 (45, D 204)

Lloyd and Marjory Rees were in Athens from 1–7 December 1959.

The Propylaia is a monumental gateway to the Acropolis erected between 437 and 432 BC. It was left incomplete at the beginning of the Peloponnesian War and work was never resumed. The Temple and bastion of Athena Nike are included in this drawing upper right.

52 *From the Acropolis, Athens* 1959

in sketchbook no. 4, p. 67
carbon pencil, watercolour 17.5 x 22.7
there is an indecipherable part-impression of a mirror-image of the inscribed title, from
the original facing page (now missing) upper left (the inscription in pen and black ink
'DELPHI' on facing p. 66 refers to the missing drawing)

Visible in this drawing is the Church of the Holy Apostles and behind it the Theseum. Lloyd and Marjory Rees visited the Acropolis three times during their week in Athens.

53 *Coast of Calabria, Italy* 1959

in sketchbook no. 4, p. 83
carbon pencil, watercolour 17.5 x 22.7
inscribed in pen and black ink 'COAST OF CALABRIA' on facing p. 82 lower left

Lloyd and Marjory Rees left for Sicily from Brindisi. As Rees wrote of the experience to his son and daughter-in-law on 11 December 1959 from Taormina, Sicily:

"The trip round from Brindisi to Messina was quite a picnic. 7am train to Taranto where we changed into another taking the coastline right round the foot to Reggio. Had gone about 20 miles when we were stopped & told to get out. In great confusion, altho' helped much by a little fat conductor (who carried our luggage) we were all bundled into an overcrowded bus & set off over rather rough roads (myself standing). We soon found the reason. Floods had washed the line away! And what a pitiable sight the country was. Whole farms washed into the valleys & roads broken through in all directions. When we joined the railway again after about 15 to 20 miles in the bus we only had dead slow methods at times but no further breakdowns to Reggio but naturally were late arriving at Messina."

54 *Taormina, Sicily* 1959

in sketchbook no. 4, p. 77
carbon pencil, watercolour 17.5 x 22.7
inscribed in pen and black ink 'TAORMINA SICILY' on facing p. 76 lower left; there is a part-impression in
mirror-image of the inscribed title from facing p. 76 upper left

Lloyd and Marjory Rees visited Taormina on 11 December 1959. As Rees wrote to
his son and daughter-in-law from Taormina that day:

> "We do get into some strange & exciting places! This hotel is on top of cliffs not
> unlike Bulli only the sea is immediately below. The ancient Greeks, Romans,
> Normans Arabs all seem to have coveted it & now we from Australia do
> likewise!"

1966–67

Lloyd and Marjory Rees left Sydney for Europe by ship in late July 1966. They spent the first month, from late August to late September in Italy, three weeks of which were in San Gimignano. They were in Greece and the Greek Islands from late September and to mid-October, followed by a week in Venice, before travelling to Paris and London. After two months in England and Scotland, November and December 1966, the Reeses visited Portugal and Spain, staying in Majorca for a month. In late February 1967 they were in the south of France, then again in Paris, in England and Scotland in March, before leaving for Australia by ship via the Suez Canal early in April 1967.

55 *Duomo Santa Maria del Fiore, Florence* 1966

in sketchbook no. 11, p. 21
pen and black ink, carbon pencil, watercolour 12.6 x 20.2
inscribed in pen and black ink 'Florence' above perforated tear-line upper left

Lloyd and Marjory Rees visited Florence twice in 1966, on 6 September and again
17–20 September. In her diary for 19 September Marjory Rees noted that Lloyd
Rees was attracted to the famous outlook across the city from the Piazzale
Michelangelo:

"Piazza Michelangelo where L. makes three drawings …"

56 *Study for 'Venetian Quay' (Riva Ca' di Dio)* 1966
in sketchbook no. 11, p. 31
pen and black ink, carbon pencil, watercolour 12.6 x 20.1
inscribed in carbon pencil 'VENICE' above perforated tear-line upper left and in pen and black ink 'V' lower left

Lloyd and Marjory Rees were in Venice 20–24 September 1966.

5 / *Fondamenta Zattere, Venice* 1966
from sketchbook no. 11, p. 33
pen and black ink, carbon pencil, watercolour 11.4 x 20.2
inscribed in carbon pencil 'VENICE' on the guard strip between pp. 32 and 33, left

BASSANO

58 *Bridge over the Brenta, Bassano* 1966

from sketchbook no. 11, p. 29
pen and black ink, carbon pencil, watercolour 11.5 x 20.2
inscribed in pen and black ink 'BASSANO' lower left
illustrated: *Rees drawings* 1978 p. 54 (44) as 'Bassano, Italy'

Lloyd and Marjory Rees were in Bassano on 23 September 1966 as part of a tour
of Venetian villas. A wooden bridge over the River Brenta, Ponte degli Alpini,
features in this drawing. It was designed by Andrea Palladio (1508–80) in 1569.

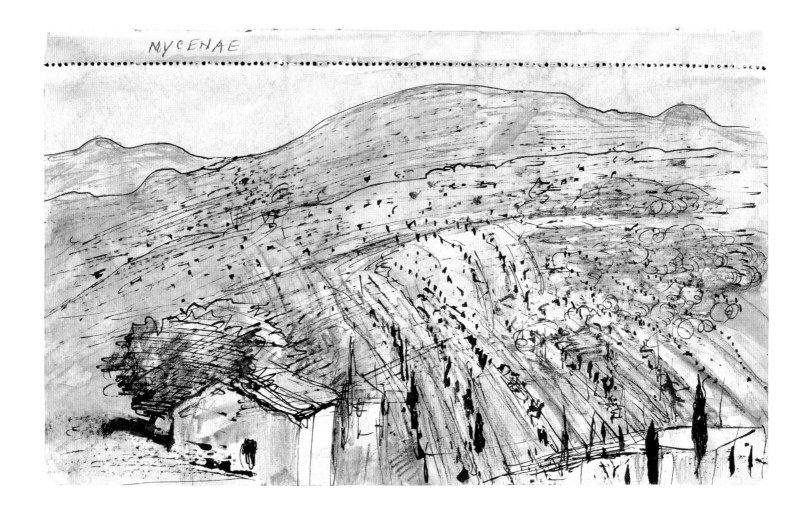

59 *Mycenae* 1966

in sketchbook no. 11, p. 51
pen and black ink, carbon pencil, watercolour 12.5 x 20.1
inscribed in black ballpoint pen 'MYCENAE' above perforated tear-line upper left

Lloyd and Marjory Rees were in Mycenae on 28 September 1966.

60 *Waterfront, Nauplion* 1966
in sketchbook no. 11, p. 57
pen and black ink, carbon pencil, watercolour 12.5 x 20.2
inscribed in black ballpoint pen 'NAUPLION' above perforated tear-line upper left

Lloyd and Marjory Rees were in Nauplion between 28 September and 2 October 1966.

In a letter to friends, Lorraine and Joe Haines on 14 October 1966, Rees wrote:

"[We] stayed at a wonderful village called Nauplion on the water overlooking plain & bay of Argos & the hotel was the most delightful we have stayed in (called the Agamemnon) with a beautiful room with a private balcony overlooking quay and the lovely bay & mountains beyond. Exquisite! Motor traffic banned from the quay, & at night tables & chairs everywhere, with people drinking & chatting till midnight & more & the little boats would pull into the quays & the fishing boats too & the little brown fishermen would sell their catch & mend their nets."

This drawing is one of six of Nauplion in sketchbook no. 11, 1966. There are some larger drawings of Nauplion in private collections – refer to *Rees drawings* AGNSW 1995 p. 75 (82) and the exhibition catalogue *Lloyd Rees, coming home* Rockhampton 1999 p. 40 (20).

61 *Nauplion* 1966

in sketchbook no. 11, p. 61
pen and black ink, carbon pencil, watercolour 12.5 x 20.1
signed with initials in carbon pencil 'LR' lower right; inscribed in black ballpoint pen 'NAUPLION' above
perforated tear-line upper left

62 *Greek Isles* 1966

in sketchbook no. 11, p. 85
pen and black ink, carbon pencil, watercolour 12.5 x 20.2
inscribed in pen and black ink 'GREEK ISLES' above perforated tear-line upper left

The Reeses were amongst the Dodecanese, the most southerly of the Greek Islands, on 6 October 1966. They were on a cruise of the southern Greek Islands, visiting Crete, Rhodes, Bodrum (in Turkey), Kos, Patmos, Delos and Mýkonos.

This drawing is the basis for the soft-ground etching *Greek Isles* 1976 from the series 'Memories of Europe' – refer to *Rees etchings and lithographs* 1986 p. 22 (4).

63 *Delos* 1966

in sketchbook no. 11, p. 91
pen and black ink, carbon pencil, watercolour 12.5 x 20.1
inscribed in pen and black ink 'DELOS' above perforated tear-line upper left

According to Marjory Rees's diary, she and Lloyd Rees visited Delos on 7 October 1966. Delos is a small uninhabited island, one of the most important archaeological sites in Greece. On 7 October she wrote:

> "6.30 Breakfast Anchor at Delos 8 am. Disembark by motor launch to visit uninhabited (except for a few shepherds, guards of archaeological treasures & staff of the Museum & tourist pavilion) & unshaded Id. Hats recommended (Woman & 2 donkeys nr wharf)."

and quoting a souvenir booklet:

> "DELOS ARCHAIC SILENT RUINED."

64 *Church on Mýkonos waterfront* 1966
in sketchbook no. 11, p. 99
pen and black ink, carbon pencil, watercolour 12.6 x 20.2
inscribed in pen and black ink 'MYCONOS' above perforated tear-line upper left

According to Marjory Rees's diary she and Lloyd Rees were on Mýkonos from 7–9 October 1966.

    This is one of 14 drawings of Mýkonos which Rees made in sketchbook no. 11, 1966, the most of any one place in this sketchbook.

65 *Kástro, Mýkonos* 1966
from sketchbook no. 11, p. 103
pen and black ink, carbon pencil, watercolour 11.4 x 20.2
inscribed in pen and black ink 'MYCONOS' on stub remaining in sketchbook, left

In this drawing can be seen one of the sixteenth century working windmills, a distinctive feature of Kástro, the oldest part of Mýkonos Town.

MYCONOS

66 *Church, Mýkonos* 1966

from sketchbook no. 11, p. 107
pen and black ink, carbon pencil, watercolour 11.4 x 20.2
signed with initials, dated in pen and black ink 'LR / 66" lower right; inscribed 'MYCONOS' on stub remaining
in sketchbook, left
illustrated: *Rees drawings* 1978 p. 61 (51) as 'Church at Mykonos, Greek Islands'

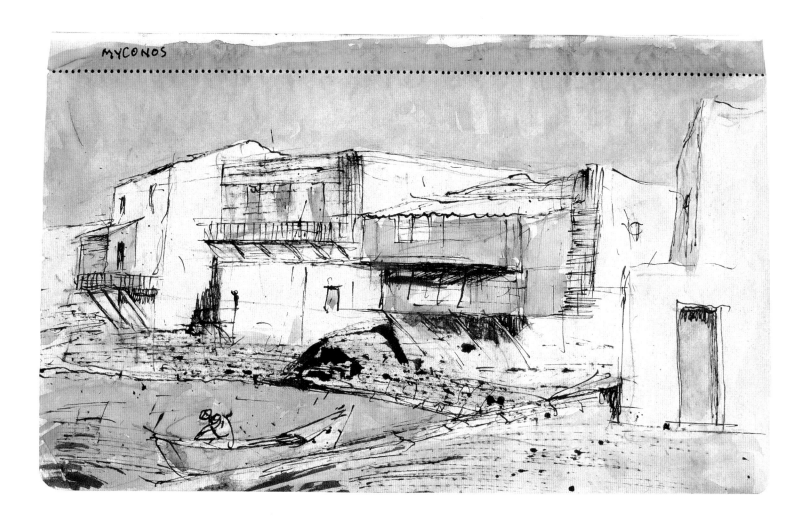

67 *Little Venice, Mýkonos* 1966
in sketchbook no. 11, p. 111
pen and black ink, carbon pencil, watercolour 12.5 x 20.2
inscribed in pen and black ink 'MYCONOS' above perforated tear-line upper left

Little Venice in Mýkonos town is known as the "artists' quarter". Its houses have painted balconies that jut out over the sea, as in Rees's drawing.

68 *Mýkonos waterfront* 1966

in sketchbook no. 11, p. 119
pen and black ink, carbon pencil, watercolour 12.4 x 20.1
inscribed in pen and black ink 'MYKONOS' above perforated tear-line upper left

As in no. 65 *Kástro, Mýkonos*, some of the remaining windmills which used to grind
corn on Mýkonos feature in this drawing.

69 *The monastery of Daphni* 1966

in sketchbook no. 11, p. 127
pen and black ink, carbon pencil, watercolour 12.4 x 20.1
inscribed in pen and black ink 'DAPHNI' above perforated tear-line upper left

This is one of three drawings Lloyd Rees made in sketchbook no. 11 of the
monastery of Daphni. According to Marjory Rees's diary, 10 October 1966:

> "Take taxi to Daphni to see mosaics – 60d + 10d Entrance fee. Byzantian
> Church restored – Lovely building with mosaics & frescoes all over interior –
> L makes 3 sketches from outside, is quite fascinated. Buy some more slides
> (Bang goes another 80dr). Ask tourist police about returning by bus".

70 *Mountains of Delphi* 1966

from sketchbook no. 11, p. 135
pen and black ink, carbon pencil, watercolour 11.3 x 20.1
inscribed in pen and black ink 'DELPHI' on stub remaining in sketchbook, left
illustrated: *Rees drawings* 1978 p. 62 (52) as 'Mountains in Greece'

According to Marjory Rees's diary she and Lloyd Rees arrived at
Hotel Vousaz, Delphi and stayed 11–12 October 1966. As she
wrote on 11 October:

> "enter lift at Ground Floor – then descend past 6, 5, 4 to 3rd
> floor. Our room 307 has wonderful private balcony over the
> valley … Lloyd is thrilled with the majesty and grandeur of the
> hills … The valley contains 2 million olive trees – just a little
> way from the Port of Itea where the Pilgrims used to land … L
> makes 3 drawings before dinner at 8pm."

On 12 October:

> "Lloyd up at daybreak drawing."

This drawing is the basis for a larger version *Delphi I* 1966 (refer
to *Rees drawings* AGNSW 1995 (85)). For Lloyd Rees's account
refer to *Later works* 1983 p. 34.

71 *Towards the Bay of Itea from Delphi* 1966

from sketchbook no. 11, p. 137
pen and black ink, carbon pencil, watercolour 11.3 x 20.2
inscribed in pen and black ink 'DELPHI' on stub remaining in sketchbook, left
illustrated: *Rees drawings* 1978 p. 59 (49) as 'Delphi I'

Rees produced a larger version of this subject *Delphi II* 1966, in a private
collection. There were five drawings of Delphi in sketchbook no. 11, all of which
Rees removed.

72 *Street in Delphi* 1966

from sketchbook no. 11, p. 139
pen and black ink, carbon pencil, wash 11.4 x 20.2
inscribed in pen and black ink 'DELPHI' on stub remaining in sketchbook, left
illustrated: *Rees drawings* 1978 p. 60 (50) as 'Delphi II'

73 *Delphi* 1966

from sketchbook no. 11, p. 141
pen and black ink, carbon pencil, watercolour 11.3 x 20.2
inscribed in pen and black ink 'DELPHI' on stub remaining in sketchbook, left

In a letter to friends Joe and Lorraine Haines dated 14 October 1966, Rees wrote:

"We found on returning to Athens we had about 4 days wait for this ship to take us back to Venice & so spent two of them on a trip to Delphi. Hotel built on edge of precipice – one entered at top & went down 6 floors in lift. Our room with balcony looked down into the immense gorge with its river winding among the mountains to the Gulf of Corinth.

On the floor of the valley [there is] supposedly the largest olive grove in Europe (two million trees!) And towering above was Mount Parnassus. What a site! In fact what a genius the Greeks had for their temples & their theatres. Imagine the superstitious going to Delphi to consult the Oracle having their bones turned to jelly when faced with such awesomeness. And then believing everything they were told!!"

74 *The canal, Torcello* 1966
from sketchbook no. 11, p. 161
carbon pencil, watercolour 11.3 x 20.1
inscribed in black ballpoint pen 'TORCELLO' on stub remaining in sketchbook, left
illustrated: *Rees drawings* 1978 p. 53 (43) as 'Torcello, Italy'.

According to Marjory Rees's diary she and Lloyd Rees visited Torcello from Venice on 18 October 1966:

> "Sun is shining so set out for Torcello & a posh lunch … We enjoyed it all & then sat in sunny garden (adorned with pomegranates) while L. did some more sketches & I wrote a few more lines … Off we set towards ferry but stop en route for some more sketches. I sit on bridge & dreamily continue writing. Back to ferry shed – another sketch & finally a quick return trip back to Venice."

This drawing is the basis for a larger drawing now in the National Gallery, Canberra – refer to *Rees drawings* AGNSW 1995 p. 79 (86).

75 *From our window, Paris* 1966
in sketchbook no. 11, p. 171
pen and black ink, carbon pencil, watercolour 12.5 x 20.1
inscribed in black ballpoint pen 'FROM OUR WINDOW – PARIS' above perforated tear-line upper left

Lloyd and Marjory Rees were in Paris from 21 October to 1 November 1966 and stayed in the same hotel on Place Dauphine as they had on their previous visit in 1959. The Pavillon de Flore and Guichet du Carrousel were clearly visible from their hotel window. Rees made a number of drawings from the window of their hotel in this sketchbook, two of which, as 'Paris I' and 'Paris II', are included in *Rees drawings* AGNSW 1995 (84).

76 *Buildings along the Quai des Orfèvres, Paris* 1966
in sketchbook no. 11, p. 181
pen and black ink, carbon pencil, watercolour 12.5 x 20.2

The hotel in which Lloyd and Marjory Rees stayed is in the first building on the
left in this drawing. It is situated on the corner of Quai des Orfèvres and Pont-
Neuf, one of the pavilions flanking the entrance to Place Dauphine directly behind
this row of buildings.

77 *Paris at night* 1966
in sketchbook no. 11, p. 185
carbon pencil, watercolour 12.4 x 20.1

This drawing featuring Pont-Neuf, is similar to a small painting *Paris* 1963 in a
private collection.

78 *Interior, Chartres Cathedral* 1966

from sketchbook no. 14, between pp. 4 and 5
pen and black ink, carbon pencil, wash
20.6 x 14.9
signed with initials, dated in pen and black ink
'L R 66' lower left; inscribed in black ballpoint
pen 'CHARTRES' on verso upper right,
referring to the drawing which would follow it
in the sketchbook

Chartres Cathedral continued to attract Rees's interest from his first visit to it. He visited the Cathedral in 1953 (twice), 1959, 1966 and in 1973 when he spent five days working almost full-time in the Cathedral.

On 14 October 1966, *en route* from Athens to Venice Rees wrote to his son and daughter-in-law:

"Will see Chartres in a matter of a week or so."

According to Marjory Rees's diary on 29 October 1966:

"Chartres – to Cathedral and windows seem lovelier than ever … L makes a drawing … then we wander off in search of lunch … L. makes a drawing of [river] bank which reminds him of Holland and then back to the Cathedral. Wander round & L. makes another sketch & falls sound asleep – I wake him at 4pm and we get our train."

79 *Interior, Chartres Cathedral* 1966

in sketchbook no. 14, p.7
pen and black ink, watercolour 20.6 x 14.9
inscribed in black ballpoint pen
'CHARTRES' on facing p. 6 lower right

80 *Eiffel Tower from the Tuileries Gardens, Paris* 1966
in sketchbook no. 14, p. 9
pen and black ink, carbon pencil, watercolour 14.9 x 20.6
inscribed in black ballpoint pen 'PARIS' on facing p. 8 lower right
illustrated: *Lloyd Rees survey, drawings and paintings 1918–1980* University Gallery, University of Melbourne
1981, p.1

The view of the Eiffel Tower in this drawing is from the Tuileries Gardens
alongside the Jeu de Paume. In her diary on 30 October 1966 Marjory Rees wrote:

> 'L. wants to sketch in Tuileries Garden, so off we go. I find sunny spot out of
> wind so settled down to write this up."

81 *Earthquake relics, Lisbon* 1967

in sketchbook no. 12, p. 33
carbon pencil, wash 13.3 x 17.8
inscribed in blue ballpoint pen 'EARTHQUAKE RELICS LISBON' on facing p. 32 lower right

In her diary for 12 January 1967, Marjory Rees noted:

"… go up to ruins of Cathedral which was destroyed by earthquake in 1775.
The Apse is now a museum – has been partly restored. We explore it all;
L. makes a sketch of the doorway, quite dramatic!"

Lisbon's great earthquake occurred in 1755. The Cathedral in this drawing is the
distinctive Church of the Carmelites.

82 *Street in Oeiras, Portugal* 1967
in sketchbook no. 12, p. 37
pen and black ink, carbon pencil, watercolour 13.3 x 17.9
inscribed in black felt pen 'OEIRAS - PORTUGAL' on facing p. 36 lower right

According to Marjory Rees, in her diary for 13 January 1967:

> "Take bus & train to OEIRAS to visit [Gulbenkian] Museum – beautiful little
> Palace … Outside most magnificent park like gardens. Find a place for lunch;
> afterwards L. keeps seeing subjects …"

83 *Granada* 1967

from sketchbook no. 15, p. 5
pen and black ink, carbon pencil, wash 19 x 25.1
signed with initials, dated in black ballpoint pen 'LR 67' lower left
illustrated: *Rees drawings* 1978 p. 67 (57) as 'Granada, Spain'

Lloyd and Marjory Rees left Lisbon on 14 January as part of a bus tour to Madrid.
They were in Granada 17–19 January and stayed overnight at the Alhambra Palace
Hotel.

84 *Moorish tower, Granada* 1967

in sketchbook no. 12, p. 55
pen and black ink, black ballpoint pen, carbon pencil, watercolour 13.3 x 17.8
inscribed in blue ballpoint pen 'GRANADA' lower right of original facing page removed from the sketchbook
(the verso of *Near Malaga, Spain*, leaving a paper strip in the spiral)

A tower in Albaicín in the old Moorish quarter, Granada.

85 *Iglesia de la Mota, Alcalá la Real, Spain* 1967

in sketchbook no. 12, p. 63
pen and black ink, black ballpoint pen, carbon pencil, wash 13.3 x 17.8
inscribed in pen and black ink 'ALCALAL REAL SPAIN' lower right, and in another hand in carbon pencil
'Alcalal Real' upper left of original facing page removed from the sketchbook (the verso of *Granada*, leaving a
paper strip in the spiral)

Alcalá la Real is on the road from Granada to Córdoba. The Moorish church in this
drawing and the ruins of the Castillo de la Mota overlook the town.

86 *Mudejar Castle, Espejo* 1967

from sketchbook no. 12 between pp. 64 and 65
pen and black ink, carbon pencil, wash 13.4 x 17.4, left serrated edge trimmed
inscribed in pen and black ink 'CORDOVA' on verso lower right, referring to the drawing which follows it, p. 65
of sketchbook no. 12 (the inscription for this drawing in pen and black ink 'ESPEJO SPAIN' is on p. 64, the verso
of *Iglesia de la Mota, Alcalá la Real, Spain*)
illustrated: *Rees drawings* 1978 p. 68 (58) as 'Castle in Spain'

After Alcalá la Real, the bus stopped at Espejo before reaching Córdoba on 19
January. Espejo is just south of Córdoba.

87 *The old town, Palma, Majorca* 1967

in sketchbook no. 12, p. 77
pen and black ink, black ballpoint pen, watercolour 13.3 x 17.9
inscribed in pen and black ink 'PALMA' on facing page lower right

Lloyd and Marjory Rees were in Palma, Majorca between 24 and 25 January, and stayed overnight at the Hotel Costa Azol.

This drawing is the basis for the soft-ground etching *Spanish Village*, refer to *Rees etchings and lithographs* 1986 p. 26 (8).

88 *Palma, Majorca* 1967
in sketchbook no. 15, p. 7
pen and black ink, carbon pencil, wash 20.1 x 25.2
signed with initials, dated in pen and black ink 'LR 67' lower left; inscribed 'PALMA MAJORCA' above
perforated tear-line upper left

89 *Plaza Soller, Majorca* 1967
in sketchbook no. 12, p. 101
black ballpoint pen, grey wash 13.4 x 17.9

Jean Bellette and her husband, Paul Haefliger, lived near Soller, Majorca. It was at their suggestion that Lloyd and Marjory Rees visited Majorca in 1967. On the recommendation of friends of the Haefligers, Norma and Lionel Gray, the Reeses rented a cottage in the village of Fornalutx, near Soller. Rees was excited at the prospect, writing from Soller on 28 January 1967 to his son and daughter-in-law:

> "If we like it I see no reason that we shouldn't stay here for most of February … & it could be a happy hunting ground for me."

On 3 February 1967 Marjory Rees wrote:

> "Waiting for us in Palma was a letter from Norma Gray telling us about these cottages in her village FORNALUTX – & a maid to do all the shopping & urging us to come out & see them. Dad fell at once for them as subject matter is ideal and he is so excited about it & works & works."

The Reeses rented the smallest and second highest cottage in Fornalutx from 29 January to 22 February 1967.

This drawing is the basis for the soft-ground etching *Plaza Soller, Majorca* 1976 from the series 'Memories of Europe' – refer to *Rees etchings and lithographs* 1986 p. 21 (3).

FORNALUTX MAJORCA

LR 67

90 *Fornalutx cottage, Majorca* 1967

in sketchbook no. 15, p. 23
black ballpoint pen, watercolour 20.2 x 25.2
signed with initials, dated in pen and black ink 'LR 67' lower left; inscribed 'FORNALUTX MAJORCA' above
perforated tear-line upper left

Lloyd and Marjory Rees stayed in Fornalutx for most of February 1967. The owner of their stone cottage was Len Harrop, Professor of Spanish at the University of New South Wales.

In a letter to Alan and Jan Rees dated 2 February 1967, Marjory Rees wrote of Fornalutx:

> "This tiny mt. village is low on the slopes of Majorca's highest peak, 8000 ft and temp. is nippy morning & evening, and we are in a cottage or "house" very reminiscent of Heath Robinson."

and on 3 February 1967:

> "This cottage is called in Spanish 'The house with the chimney' & we got a basket full of wood delivered at the front door & so we have fires every evening. Dad gets great joy in piling the wood on the fire."

Lloyd Rees was particularly attracted to the landscape at Fornalutx; as he wrote to Daphne Mayo on 10 February 1967:

> "The landscape is like a drug it is so beautiful. Not only in details such as peasant architecture & clustering villages but in great majestic forms culminating in peaks going up to 5000 feet & all within a few miles of our door."

This drawing is also the basis for the soft-ground etching *Farm house, Majorca* 1976, see *Rees etchings and lithographs* 1986 p. 24 (6). There are other drawings of the same subject – see sketchbook no. 12, 1966–67 p. 117 and *Rees drawings* AGNSW 1995 p. 79 (88).

91 *Concepcion in the kitchen, Fornalutx* 1967

in sketchbook no. 12, p 125
pen and black ink, carbon pencil, watercolour 13.3 x 17.9

This drawing shows the interior of the cottage Lloyd and Marjory Rees rented in Fornalutx. According to Marjory Rees in her letter from Fornalutx of 3 February 1967:

> "…we have a Spanish maid called Concepsion who takes the ashes out of our fireplace & buys something to cook for our Spanish lunch every day."

92 *Cottage with washing line, Fournalutx* 1967

in sketchbook no. 12, p. 119
pen and black ink, carbon pencil, watercolour 13.3 x 17.9

This drawing is the basis for the soft-ground etching *Majorca* 1976, see *Rees etchings and lithographs* 1986 p. 30 (12).

According to Marjory Rees's diary on 2 February 1967:

"Do a little washing including L's heavy woollen underclothes and have the great joy of pegging them out to dry in the sunshine, on a line on our own lower patio".

93 *Puig Mayor, Fornalutx* 1967

in sketchbook no. 13, p. 1
carbon pencil, watercolour 25.2 x 35.3
signed with initials, dated in black ballpoint pen 'LR / 67' lower left; inscribed 'FORNALUTX→' on facing
inside front cover lower right

In a letter to Daphne Mayo dated 10 February 1967, Marjory Rees wrote:

> "I've been writing lies (all unknowing) to my friends saying the mountain
> we see is 8000ft high (so we were told). But its true height is only 5000ft.
> But today there was plenty of snow on it."

and in her diary of 12 February she wrote:

> "Cold & wet, 3rd day of snow on mts. especially The Pooch, i.e. El Puig
> which is the highest pt. about 5000ft."

94 *Olive and orange groves, Fornalutx, Majorca* 1967

in sketchbook no. 15, p. 39
pen and black ink, carbon pencil, watercolour 20.2 x 25.2
signed with initials, dated in pen and black ink 'LR 67' lower left; inscribed 'FORNALUTX MAJORCA' above
perforated tear-line upper left

There is a larger related drawing *Moorish terraces, Majorca* 1967 in the National
Gallery of Victoria.

95 *Farmhouses, Fornalutx*

in sketchbook no. 15, p. 43
pen and black ink, carbon pencil, wash 20.2 x 25.2
signed with initials, dated in black ballpoint pen 'LR / 67' lower left; inscribed 'FARM HOUSES FORNALUTX'
above perforated tear-line upper left

96 *Cart, Majorca* 1967
in sketchbook no. 12, p. 91
carbon pencil, watercolour 13.3 x 17.9

A similar cart appears in a major drawing *Tuscan landscape with San Gimignano*
1966 in the AGNSW collection; refer to *Rees drawings* AGNSW 1995 p. 76 (83).

97 *River Orb from St. Nazaire, Béziers* 1967

from sketchbook no. 14, between pp. 12 and 13, and attached to *River with ford, Béziers*
black felt pen, watercolour 15 x 20.2
illustrated: Free *Rees* 1972 p. 124 (D298); *Rees drawings* 1978 p.70 (60) as 'The river, Béziers, France'

Lloyd and Marjory Rees visited Béziers in Languedoc, southern France, at the end
of February and stayed five days. Rees made a number of drawings from St. Nazaire
in Béziers, the basis of his painting *A tribute to France* 1968–69. While in Béziers,
the Reeses visited the Australian artist Fred Jessup, who still lives nearby at Servian.

98 *Study for 'A tribute to France'* 1967

from sketchbook no. 13, between pp. 2 and 3 (i)
pen and black ink, carbon pencil, watercolour 25.2 x 35.3
signed with initials, dated in black ballpoint pen 'LR 67' lower right; inscribed in black ballpoint pen
'BEZIERS, FRANCE →' on verso referring to the drawing which would follow it in the sketchbook
illustrated: 'Special gifts' *Art Gallery of New South Wales Quarterly* Volume 12, no. 4, July 1971 p. 622

Lloyd Rees gave this drawing to the AGNSW in 1971 to complement its
purchase of his major painting *A tribute to France* 1968–69. It is one of seven
known drawings related to the painting. Three drawings are from sketchbook
no. 13, 1967 (one of which is in the collection of the National Gallery,
Canberra), three are from sketchbook no. 14, 1966–67, a larger seventh
drawing is in a private collection.

99 *The fields of Béziers* 1967
from sketchbook no. 13, between pp. 2 and 3 (ii)
pen and black ink, carbon pencil, watercolour 25.2 x 34.7, left serrated edge trimmed
signed with initials, dated in black ballpoint pen 'LR 67' lower left; inscribed in black felt pen 'YORKS→'/
FORNALUTX→/ and in black ballpoint pen, deleted in black felt pen 'NEAR HUDDERSFIELD,
YORKS→' on verso referring to the drawing which would follow it in the sketchbook
illustrated: Free *Rees* 1972 p. 124 (D297); *Rees drawings* 1978 p. 71 (61) as 'Farmlands, Béziers, France'

This is one of Lloyd Rees's studies for his painting *A tribute to France* 1968–69
in the AGNSW collection.

100 *Modern Naples* 1967

in sketchbook no. 14, p. 19
black ballpoint pen, carbon pencil, watercolour 15 x 20.7
inscribed in black ballpoint pen 'NAPLES' on facing page lower right
illustrated: *Lloyd Rees survey; drawings and paintings 1918–1980* University Gallery, University of Melbourne
1981, inside back cover

Lloyd and Marjory Rees left Europe from Southampton, England on 5 April 1967
on board the Achille Lauro, which sailed to Australia via the Suez Canal. The ship
called at Genoa, Naples, Messina and Malta. In each place Rees drew in his
sketchbooks.

101 *Castel Nuovo and Museo Nazionale di San Martino, Naples* 1967

in sketchbook no. 13, p. 13
black ballpoint pen, carbon pencil, watercolour 25.2 x 35.3
signed with initials, dated in black ballpoint pen 'LR / 67' lower left; inscribed 'NAPLES→' on facing
page lower right

Other versions of the subject are in sketchbook no. 2, 1953, p. 15, sketchbook
no. 3, 1953, p. 71, and sketchbook no. 13, 1967, p. 15.

102 *Street in Valletta, Malta* 1967
in sketchbook no. 14, p. 25
pen and black ink, ballpoint pen, watercolour 15 x 20.7
inscribed in black ballpoint pen 'VALETTA MALTA→' on facing page lower right

On their return to Australia by ship, Lloyd and Marjory Rees had a day in Malta on
12 April 1967.

103 *Valletta, Malta* 1967
in sketchbook no. 15, p. 55
pen and black ink, black ballpoint pen, carbon pencil, watercolour
20.2 x 25.1
signed with initials, dated in black ballpoint pen 'LR 67' lower right;
inscribed 'VALETTA MALTA' above perforated tear-line upper left

This drawing evokes what Rees wrote about Malta to Alan and
Jan Rees on 22 May 1959 on the previous visit:

"Malta an extraordinary place – so glad we've seen it. A poem
in stone – hardly any growing thing to be seen from water.
Beautifully built & of lovely colour from cream to brown pink
& little casements to tell of Moorish influence."

104 *Plains of Egypt* 1967
in sketchbook no. 15, p. 63
pen and black ink, black ballpoint pen, carbon pencil, watercolour 20.1 x 25.1
signed with initials in black ballpoint pen 'LR/67' lower left; inscribed 'EGYPT' above
perforated tear-line upper left

The Achille Lauro, the ship on which Lloyd and Marjory Rees
were returning to Australia, sailed through the Suez Canal in April
1967. Another drawing of Egypt by Rees is in the National
Gallery, Canberra. It would have followed as p. 65 of sketchbook
no. 15, 1967.

105 *Waterfront, Port Said* 1967
in sketchbook no. 15, p. 59
black ballpoint pen, carbon pencil, watercolour 20 x 25.1
signed with initials, dated in black ballpoint pen '67 LR' lower right; inscribed 'PORT SAID' above perforated
tear-line upper left

106 *Aden* 1967

in sketchbook no. 14, p. 39
pen and black ink, carbon pencil, watercolour 15 x 20.6
inscribed in black ballpoint pen 'ADEN→' on facing page lower right
illustrated: *Lloyd Rees survey, drawings and paintings 1918–1980* University Gallery, University
of Melbourne, 1981, p. 9

In a letter to Alan and Jan Rees dated 18 April 1967 and headed
'Approaching Aden', Marjory Rees wrote:

"Dad is out on a sheltered deck sketching. He must have literally
hundreds and hundreds of drawings, enough for many exhibitions
and I am happy to say all done very quickly."

107 *Aden waterfront* 1967
in sketchbook no. 15, p. 71
pen, brush and black ink, carbon pencil, watercolour 20.2 x 25.2
signed, with initials, dated in black ballpoint pen 'LR / 67' lower left; inscribed 'ADEN' above perforated tear-line
upper left

1973

Lloyd and Marjory Rees travelled to England in order to attend his first London exhibition at the New Grafton Gallery 13 September – 10 October 1973. They left Sydney by air, their first ever aeroplane flight on 20 May 1973. The first month was spent in London before leaving for Paris on 21 June. They spent five days in Chartres, where Lloyd Rees drew the interior of the Cathedral each day, and a fortnight in Vézelay in Burgundy, France. From France they travelled to Venice and San Gimignano (where they stayed a month) before returning to London for the opening of his exhibition on 12 September. They left London for Australia on 20 September 1973.

108 *Column, interior of Chartres*
Cathedral 1973

in sketchbook no. 18, p. 5
black ballpoint pen, carbon pencil, watercolour
20.2 x 13.9

Lloyd and Marjory Rees spent five days
in Chartres in July 1973. Rees drew the
interior of the Cathedral intensively on
each of those five days, drawings which
formed the basis to an extensive series
of paintings and drawings, most of
which were acquired by the University
of Sydney in 1977.

109 *Sainte-Madeleine, Vézelay* 1973
in sketchbook no. 18, p. 1
black ballpoint pen, carbon pencil, watercolour 13.9 x 20.2

After their 5 days in Chartres, Lloyd and Marjory Rees visited
Vézelay and stayed for two weeks from 13-26 July 1973.
This drawing is a study for a larger drawing in a private collection
and one of a number he made of the pilgrimage church at
Vézelay. A major oil of Vézelay is in the Art Gallery of Western
Australia, Perth.

In an undated transcript of an interview conducted by Renée Free
(AGNSW files), Rees spoke of Vézelay as:

> "This great building captured the imagination because it goes
> back so far in history, a great monastery … The rear view is
> terrifically impressive because of the strength of the buttresses
> and these tight chapels sort of harnessing it all together … The
> work I did there – the more serious work was connected with
> the basilica itself … the front view of the façade and then …
> the choir or apse to the back of the Cathedral …"

110 *Walled town, Vézelay* 1973
in sketchbook no. 18, p. 13
black ballpoint pen, carbon pencil, watercolour 13.9 x 20.2

As Rees told Renée Free (see commentary to previous drawing):

"I remember going up on to the hill – it's a hill town … and looking around this very matured landscape – very rhythmical because mankind had moved over it for centuries … a little township … nestled into the landscape so perfectly … The delightful nature of the town of course captivated us … It was a remarkable experience in that the landscape didn't have many notes – the whole thing was so simple."

Rees sketchbooks in the Gallery's collection

Sketchbook no. 1 1913–14

88 pages with drawings, variously in pencil, pen and black ink
118 pages sewn and bound between black morocco covered card covers 19.4 x 27.2, page size

This is Lloyd Rees's earliest extant sketchbook. The book was a gift from Wal Taylor, bookbinder and work-mate at the Queensland Government Printing Office, Brisbane, where Rees worked 1913–15. It has numerous studies of early Brisbane landmarks – churches, bridges and various public buildings.

Sketchbook no. 2 1953

83 pages with drawings, variously in pencil, carbon pencil, black and grey wash
'Navigating Officer's Note Book': 168 pages sewn and bound between yellow cloth covered card covers with a sleeve for a pencil 10.1 x 16.1, page size

This is Lloyd Rees's first European sketchbook. It begins with a number of drawings in Singapore (*en route* to Europe by ship), the remainder are of France, Italy and Britain. It also has nine pages of written observations of paintings in public galleries and of the Folies Bergères, Paris.

Sketchbook no. 3 1953

36 pages with drawings, variously in carbon pencil, grey wash
'Esquisse' no. 1105: 152 pages spiral bound with card covers 13.5 x 18, page size

Drawings of Italy and France.

Sketchbook no. 4 1959

48 pages with drawings, variously in carbon pencil, watercolour, pen and black ink
'Ideal Botany Exercise Book': 96 pages sewn and bound between card covers 22.7 x 17.5, page size

Drawings predominantly of Italy; also of Malta, Austria, France, Greece and the Suez Canal. One drawing of Pont St.-Michel from this sketchbook is detached. It is from between pp. 28 and 29.

Sketchbook no. 5 1959

58 pages with drawings, variously in carbon pencil, watercolour, black and grey wash, pen and blue ink, blue ballpoint pen
'Esquisse' no. 1105: 112 pages spiral bound with card covers 13.5 x 18, page size

The first fifteen drawings are of Werri on the south coast of New South Wales where Lloyd and Marjory Rees had half-share in a holiday house. These could have been made on their return from Europe in January 1954 or at any time between their 1953 and 1959 trips, or since. This sketchbook is the same as sketchbook no. 3 and was possibly bought at the same time. The remaining drawings are predominantly of Italy; also of Crete, Malta, Austria, France. Six of the drawings removed by Rees remained with this sketchbook.

Sketchbook no. 6 1959

10 pages with drawings, variously in carbon pencil, watercolour, black ballpoint pen
'Lucesa Spiral block': 88 pages spiral bound with card covers 20.8 x 14.9, page size

Drawings of Greece, Corfu, Sicily and Suez Canal. There is one drawing of Werri Beach on the south coast of New South Wales and two ballpoint pen figure studies, a draft of a letter to former NSW Premier Neville Wran dated '25.10.78' and an amateurish drawing in another hand. One drawing of Athens is attached to the detached front cover.

Sketchbook no. 7 1959

24 pages with drawings, variously in carbon pencil, watercolour, black ballpoint pen, pen and black ink, wash
'New D. Chrisikopoulos: 98 pages spiral bound with card covers 15 x 20.8, page size

Drawings of Greece and Italy; three drawings made in Hobart c. 1968 on and from Mount Wellington. There is also a draft of a letter to William Dobell dated 16.6.66.

Sketchbook no. 8 1960s

4 pages with drawings, variously in carbon pencil, grey wash
'Lucesa Spiral block': 96 pages spiral bound with card covers 20.8 x 15, page size

Drawings of Werri on the south coast of New South Wales. Included is a sheet of Grade 4 sandpaper cut to page size, which Rees used under the page on which he was drawing, in order to create a texture and to interrupt the otherwise smooth flow of his line.

Sketchbook no. 9 1960s

10 pages with drawings, variously in carbon pencil, watercolour
'New D. Chrisikopoulos: 82 pages spiral bound with card covers 29.5 x 19.6, page size

Drawings of Sydney, Werri and Tasmania.

Sketchbook no. 10 1960s

11 pages with drawings, variously in carbon pencil, watercolour, black felt pen, grey wash
'New D. Chrisikopoulos: 88 pages spiral bound with card covers 29.5 x 19.6, page size

Drawings of Sydney, Werri and of the figure.

Sketchbook no. 11 1966

66 pages and covers with drawings, variously in pen and black ink, black ballpoint pen, watercolour, carbon pencil
'Winsor and Newton, series 34': 192 pages sewn and bound in maroon covered card covers 20.3 x 12.6, page size

Drawings of Italy, Greece, Paris and the Suez Canal. There is also one of Sydney and written observations about the Venice Biennale. Twenty of the leaves removed by Rees remain with this sketchbook.

Sketchbook no. 2

Sketchbook no. 4

Sketchbook no. 18

Sketchbook no. 12 1966–67

68 pages with drawings, variously in pen and black ink, black ballpoint pen, carbon pencil, watercolour
'Esquisse' no. 1105: 132 pages spiral bound with card covers 13.3 x 17.8, page size

Drawings of England, Spain, Portugal and Majorca. Five pages were removed by Rees but remained with the sketchbook.

Sketchbook no. 13 1967

14 pages and back cover with drawings, variously in pencil, carbon pencil, black ballpoint pen and felt pen, watercolour
Winsor and Newton series 28: 24 pages spiral bound with card covers 25.2 x 35.3, page size

Drawings of Majorca, Béziers, Britain, Italy and Suez Canal. Among the drawings removed by Rees, one remains with the sketchbook. Another he gave to the Gallery in 1971 as a study for the painting *A tribute to France* 1968–69 (purchased by the Gallery in 1969).

Sketchbook no. 14 1966–67

23 pages with drawings, variously in pen and black ink, black ballpoint pen, carbon pencil, watercolour
'Lucesa spiral block': 74 pages, spiral bound with card covers 20.6 x 14.9, page size

Drawings of France, England, Italy, Malta and Suez Canal. Four pages removed by Rees remain with the sketchbook.

Sketchbook no. 15 1967

60 pages with drawings, variously in pen and black ink, carbon pencil and watercolour
'Winsor & Newton': 224 pages sewn and bound in maroon covered card covers 25.1 x 20, page size

Drawings of Spain, Majorca, Scotland, Italy, Malta, Suez Canal and Tasmania. Four of the drawings Rees removed remain with the sketchbook. A sheet of 0 grade carborundum emery cloth, cut to page size, is with the sketchbook. Rees used this under the page he was drawing on, in order to create a texture and to interrupt the otherwise smooth flow of his line.

Sketchbook no. 16 1960s–80s

17 pages with drawings, variously in carbon pencil, black ballpoint pen, oil pastel, watercolour
'Croquis Dessin no. 1746': 18 pages spiral bound with card covers 32 x 24.1, page size

Landscape drawings in Australia including Sydney Opera House and one drawing by a child.

Sketchbook no. 17 1973

17 pages with drawings, variously in black ballpoint pen, pen and black ink, carbon pencil, watercolour
'Navigating Officer's Note Book': 154 pages sewn and bound between yellow cloth covered card covers with a sleeve for a pencil 10.1 x 15.8, page size

Drawings of Chartres and Vézelay. One detached drawing remains with the sketchbook.

Sketchbook no. 18 1973

8 pages with drawings, variously in black ballpoint pen, carbon pencil, watercolour
'Wire O sketchbook': 16 pages, spiral bound with card covers 13.9 x 20.2, page size

Drawings of Vézelay and Chartres.

Sketchbook no. 19 1980s

4 pages with drawings, variously in black lithographic crayon, oil pastel, watercolour
'Spirax no. 534': 40 pages spiral bound A4 cartridge with card covers 21 x 29.7, page size

Drawings for 'New lithographs 1982'.

A working catalogue of all the drawings in the sketchbooks, including any removed which have been located in other collections, is being prepared for access via the Internet.

Acknowledgements

The greatest debt is to Alan and Jancis Rees for the gift of Lloyd Rees's remaining sketchbooks and for their assistance in researching Rees's visits to Europe, access to correspondence, Marjory Rees's travel diaries and the loan of works related to the sketchbooks. I am also grateful for their reading of the text.

A particular thanks to lenders, public and private, of works borrowed for the accompanying exhibition and to the staff who assisted in the realization of this publication and the exhibition, especially – Edmund Capon, Director; Anne Flanagan, Manager of Exhibitions; Rosemary Peel, Paper Conservator; Bill Lamont and Yandong Yang, Mountcutters; Jenni Carter, Senior Gallery Photographer; Mark Boxshall, Graphic Designer; Anne Ryan, Assistant Curator of Australian Prints, Drawings and Watercolours; Administration, Library, Registration and Installation staff. Thanks also to Simon Cuthbert for his attention to Alan Rees's photographs of his parents in Europe in 1953, to Natalie Hartog, Elizabeth Fairleigh, Peter Kothe and Nick Mourtzakis for their help at various times with Rees research; and to Jill Sykes editor of *Look* for her advice. A special thanks to Patricia James, my volunteer for the last twelve years, who has searched out and identified many of the places Lloyd Rees drew in Europe, aided in the determination of the original position of loose sketchbook drawings and assisted me throughout this project.